THE POETRY OF
WILLIAM BUTLER YEATS

SANDRA GILBERT
DEPARTMENT OF ENGLISH
STATE UNIVERSITY OF NEW YORK

D0162546

MONARCH PRESS

*We wish to thank The Macmillan Company for
permission to publish this literature guide and for
the use of brief quotations from THE POETRY OF
WILLIAM BUTLER YEATS throughout this book.*

*Published by
MONARCH PRESS
a Simon & Schuster division of
Gulf & Western Corporation
Simon & Schuster Building
1230 Avenue of the Americas
New York, N.Y. 10020*

*MONARCH PRESS and colophon are trademarks
of Simon & Schuster, registered in the U.S. Patent
and Trademark Office.*

Standard Book Number: 0-671-00738-6

Library of Congress Catalog Card Number: 65-27736

Printed in the United States of America

CONTENTS

INTRODUCTION

He sought the intensity of streams,
the foam that seems the will of stones,
the icy rush that is not dreams,
the trees that shape the path like bones . . .

Cold blood, cold blood of mountainsides,
cold blood that swells the shores, cold tides,
what truth has he found Under-Sea?
What blackness, or what clarity?
                    A. L. Purdy, "W. B. Y., d. 1939"

BACKGROUND AND CHILDHOOD: William Butler Yeats
was born in Dublin in 1865, one of a family of five children, two
girls and three boys (one of whom died in childhood while the
poet's remaining brother Jack grew up to become a fairly well
known artist). John Butler Yeats, his father, was a precariously
successful painter, as well as an intellectual, a skeptic, an agnostic,
and a wit. His mother, Susan Pollexfen Yeats, came of an old
Anglo-Irish family which, though originally from Devon, England
(his father, too, was originally English), had been important in
Sligo, in the west of Ireland, for some generations. Unlike her
husband, Mrs. Yeats was a quiet, religious woman of deep,
intuitive feelings, who loved best to spend her time exchanging
ghost and fairy stories with the peasants around Sligo.

In 1874 the Yeats family moved to London, though young Yeats
himself continued to spend a good deal of time with his grand-
parents in Sligo, where he developed much of his feeling for the
Irish countryside—the peasants, the songs and stories, the lonely
shores and the bare, wind-haunted hills. In London, from 1874
to 1883, J. B. Yeats, and through him his children, moved in some
of the best artistic circles of the day. He was friendly or acquainted
with such leading pre-Raphaelites as William Morris and Burne-
Jones, and the family lived in Bedford Park, at that time a kind
of avant-garde housing development, famous intellectual suburb
designed and lived in by a number of the most important pre-
Raphaelites and their disciples.

EDUCATION AND YOUNG MANHOOD: In 1883, when he
left high school in Dublin, Yeats decided—against his father's
wishes—not to go on to Trinity College but instead to become
an artist. He was enrolled, therefore, in the Metropolitan Art
School, where he soon discovered, perhaps with some prodding

5

from his new friend George Russell (later the poet AE), that what had hitherto been an avocation, poetry, was more important to him than his chosen vocation. By 1885 his first published poems had appeared in *The Dublin University Review*, and soon after that he began to come under the influence of the Irish nationalist leader, John O'Leary, one of the guiding spirits of the Irish Renaissance which was soon to flower so brilliantly in Dublin. In the meantime, Yeats, George Russell and a few other friends, founded the Dublin Hermetic Society, a kind of club devoted to occult research—to studies of spiritualism, magic, theosophy, esoteric Buddhism and the Cabbala. Many such organizations were flourishing in this period, and by the time he was fifty Yeats had substantially acquainted himself with the activities of them all. He joined Madame Blavatsky's Theosophical Society in 1888, the Order of the Golden Dawn in 1890, and later regularly participated in sèances.

LONDON AND "THE RHYMERS' CLUB":   By 1889, when his first book, *The Wanderings of Oisin*, was published with the help of John O'Leary, Yeats had returned more or less permanently to London, where he soon became deeply involved in current literary society. Yeats was shy and dreamy but ambitious. He and his father believed he was "destined for greatness." He forced himself to attend intellectual gatherings and to participate in all sorts of meetings and clubs. In this period, which he has vividly described in his *Autobiography*, he met such notables as Wilde, Henley and Stevenson, and in 1891, with friends of his own age —Lionel Johnson, Ernest Dowson and others—he founded the Rhymers' Club, which met weekly at the famous old London tavern, *The Cheshire Cheese*, to discuss the latest work of all its members. One of Yeats' most important literary friends in these years was the poet-critic Arthur Symons, who introduced him to many of the exciting new aesthetic ideas that were then being produced in France by poets like Mallarme, Verlaine and Villiers de L'Isle-Adam. (Arthur Symons' *The Symbolist Movement in Literature*, still an excellent lucid discussion of French symbolism, was published in 1899 and dedicated to Yeats.)

MAUD GONNE AND OLIVIA SHAKESPEAR: In 1889 Yeats met the great romantic love of his life, the beautiful actress and nationalist Maud Gonne, who was sent to him with a letter of introduction (she admired his first book of poems, which had just been published) by John O'Leary. For the next twenty years he devoted himself to wooing her, and, too, devoted much of his poetry to praising her (cf. Introduction to *The Wind Among The Reeds*), yet all in vain. Maud Gonne apparently felt that Yeats was too dreamy, too idealistic, to be the right husband for her.

And though he passionately exerted himself to become the kind of active political man she admired, in 1903 she married Major John MacBride, dealing a terrible death-blow to the poet's hopes, from which he never recovered. Indeed, though Madame MacBride was shortly (in 1905) separated from her husband, the old romantic glow was gone, both from their relationship and from Yeats' work. As time went by, his style became increasingly bitter and spare; turning more and more to drama, he stripped away the elaborate, ornate imagery with which he had decorated his early love poems and began to write harder, terser, more epigrammatic poems, dealing mainly with politics and metaphysics.

During some of the time that he was wooing Maud Gonne, however, Yeats became involved with another woman, a young, beautiful married woman named Olivia Shakespear who, meeting him in 1894 in the literary circles of the day, fell in love with him and agreed to go away with him. Though their affair seems to have lasted about a year, it ended badly. Mrs. Shakespear discovered that Yeats was really still in love with Maud Gonne and, deeply wounded, left him. Years later when, reconciled, she had become one of his dearest confidantes and correspondents, Yeats wrote to her: "I came upon two early photographs of you yesterday, while going through my file . . . Who ever had a like profile? —a profile from a Sicilian coin. One looks back to one's youth as to [a] cup that a mad man dying of thirst left half tasted. I wonder if you feel like that."

THE ABBEY THEATRE: In 1899 Yeats, with George Moore, Edward Martyn, and his patroness, Lady Augusta Gregory, founded the Irish theatrical society which was eventually to become the world-famous Abbey Theatre. This organization first staged the plays of such major Irish playwrights as Lady Gregory, John Synge, Sean O'Casey, and, of course, Yeats himself. Yeats' plays, though not his most significant literary achievement, were extremely successful in their day, especially *The Countess Cathleen* and *Cathleen ni Houlihan*, both works infused with Irish nationalist fervor. More important, his long experience with play-writing and with other "theatre business" helped, as we have noted, to simplify his ornate early style, making it more precise, more dramatic, more conversational. And the experience with "management of men" that the Abbey work entailed—like his long political involvement—helped to counterbalance his mysticism and dreaminess, to root his work solidly and deeply in the reality which he increasingly came to look upon as the ultimate source of art.

MARRIAGE AND A *VISION*:   After years of lonely bachelorhood, of futile courtship of Maud Gonne, and of other unhappy love affairs, Yeats found himself at fifty still childless and unmarried. Frustrated and unhappy, he set out to remedy the situation. After being turned down again by Maud Gonne, and—worse—by her beautiful adopted daughter, Iseult (who was some thirty years the poet's junior), he finally married a vivacious, intelligent young lady to whom Ezra Pound and Olivia Shakespear had introduced him: Miss Georgie Hyde-Lees. The pair settled down to a married life spent (for a while) between Oxford and Dublin. Then they took to living (at least in the summers) at the old farmhouse and tower of Thoor Ballylee. Yeats had bought this property from Lady Gregory, whose own estate (Coole Park, were the poet had summered for many years) adjoined it.

Shortly after their marriage, when Yeats was feeling despondent (cf. Introduction to *The Wild Swans at Coole*), Mrs. Yeats, to distract him, began trying her hand at automatic writing. The ideas and images she came up with were so exciting to the poet (whose fascination with the occult, as we have seen, dated from early youth) that he developed them into an esoteric system of his own, *A Vision*, which he published in 1925 (and in revised form in 1937). This elaborate, semi-astrological work contains five sections (five Books, plus prefatory material, as well as a verse prologue and epilogue). The first two sections deal with a kind of astrological character-analysis, based on the phases of the moon rather than on the stars. Men are divided into two types, primary and antithetical (defined elsewhere in this book), according to a complex system which positions them on the Great Wheel of the moon's monthly journey. Book Three deals with "the soul in judgment," with the process of the afterlife whereby it spins away its "mortal coil"—the lunar-influenced incarnation of its earthly existence—and returns to "breathless" cosmic darkness, to timeless union with the absolute. Finally, Books Four and Five shift from the earlier concern with the wheels and cycles in which individual lives may run, and turn to an analysis of the larger scene, setting forth an elaborate cyclical theory of history which was based partly on Renaissance and Neoplatonist doctrines and which seemed partly to parallel, in the circular "gyring" shape it imposed on man's general progress, the wheels and cones through which the poet saw particular men moving. (This kind of cyclical theory of history was also, interestingly enough, advocated by the German philosopher-historian Oswald Spengler, whose theories were translated into English between 1926 and 1929, shortly after Yeats' first version of *A Vision* was published.)

Many critics consider thorough knowledge of *A Vision* essential to a complete understanding of the poems which Yeats wrote during or after his construction of "the system." Others, however, have argued that the poems for the most part can be read independently, that though much of Yeats' imagery is traceable to *A Vision*, it is still self-explanatory within the context of the works themselves. This writer has tried to steer a middle course between these two points of view. Where *A Vision* is obviously of central importance (as, especially, in a few of the poems from *The Wild Swans at Coole*, *Michael Robartes and the Dancer*, *The Tower* and *The Winding Stair*), it has been discussed as fully as seems necessary. But in all cases an effort has been made to regard poems as, wherever possible, self-contained. Thus, though an image may be related to "the system," if it can be explained and appreciated without that system, it has been so explained. Yeats himself, after all, declared that his spiritual "instructors" had come to bring him "metaphors for poetry," and it seems plain enough, therefore, that he meant "the system" to be an adjunct to the poetry, and not the poetry an appendage to "the system."

SUCCESS, LAST YEARS AND DEATH: By 1922 Yeats was so famous and successful (though what are probably his two greatest books—*The Tower*, 1928, and *The Winding Stair*, 1933—had not yet been published) that he was appointed a Senator of the newly established Irish Free State, a capacity in which he served until 1928. He took the job seriously and assiduously supported both the arts and the aristocracy, in keeping with most of the political and historical theories he expressed in his poems. In 1924, too, he was awarded the Nobel Prize, an honor which moved him greatly. To celebrate the occasion he even wrote a little book, *The Bounty of Sweden*, praising the nobility of the Nobel Committee, and expressing his gratitude to the friends living and dead, like Augusta Gregory and John Synge, who had helped shape his career.

In his last years Yeats suffered from heart and lung conditions, a "nervous breakdown" and general physical weakness and debilitation. Yet his mind, as he himself wrote, remained as "passionate" and "fantastical" as ever Indeed, though increasingly plagued with weakness and shortness of breath, he wrote many of his greatest poems in this period. In 1934, he underwent the famous Steinach operation for rejuvenation through monkey glands. (See Aldous Huxley's *After Many a Summer Dies the Swan* for a satirical comment on this sort of operation, which was so popular in the thirties). Yeats responded to the treatment with an incredible burst of creative energy. Just five months before his death in 1939, he completed one of his greatest poems, "Under Ben Bulben," a kind of poetic last will and testament in which he outlines for the last time, in brilliantly terse lines and stanzas, some of his most important ideas on history, art and politics. In section 5 he addresses his last advice to the artists who will come after him: "Irish poets, learn your trade." W. B. Yeats himself had learned his trade as a very young man, and he never forgot it.

THE POEMS: Most of the important background material on Yeats—the details of his Platonism, his politics, his mysticism, his love affairs, his marriage, etc.—properly belongs with the poems, so that each subject can be dealt with as it arises naturally, in the course of an analysis of the *Collected Poems*. Students are advised, therefore, to read the book from beginning to end, consecutively, in order to most fully appreciate the nature of Yeats' poetic and intellectual development. Yeats' literary career was an extraordinary one, one which has been divided by critics variously into three, four and five phases, and to see most clearly the ways in which these phases succeed each other a reader must certainly start with *Crossways* and read (or at least skim) through to *Last Poems*. The ornate, dreamy, highly decorated style of *Crossways*, *The Rose*, *The Wind Among the Reeds* and *In the Seven Woods* (phase 1) gives way, he will notice, in *The Green Helmet* and *Responsibilities* (phase 2) to a terser, drier, more conversational style. The love poems give way to political poems, the songs and ballads to epigrams. Then, in *The Wild Swans at Coole*, *Michael Robartes and the Dancer*, *The Tower* and the first half of *The Winding Stair* (phase 3) the style becomes more elaborate again, though with a precision that was lacking earlier. The tone of the poems is metaphysical, but with a bitterly personal intensity and passion derived, perhaps, from the new realism of the second phase. Finally, in the second half of *The Winding Stair* and in *From "A Full Moon in March"* and *Last Poems* (phase 4) style is stripped to the bone again and, casting off many of the visionary symbols of phase 3, the poet awakens in old age into "the desolation of reality." Yet he faces this desolation with a kind of heroic gaiety (cf. Summary of *Last Poems*) and, as with everything else he encountered, he makes great art out of it.

THE COLLECTED POEMS:
SUMMARY AND COMMENT

A WORD OF WARNING: Perhaps the most important thing to remember about Yeats' major work, his *Collected Poems*, is that though the poems are arranged by "books," in roughly chronological order, in many cases the poetry, especially the early work, does not appear as Yeats originally wrote it. Yeats, as we have already noted, was a tireless and brilliant reviser. He revised his verses ceaselessly and re-arranged them with endless craftsmanlike care. Furthermore, he skillfully linked poem to poem, not in the order in which they were written, but in the order of their aesthetic logic, the order in which each would show to the greatest advantage, like variegated jewels on a chain. His *Collected Poems* is thus almost a single work, a necklace of meditations, a kind of intricate epic of the poet's mind, reflecting in all its moods on reality as it presented itself to him.

In dealing with this formidable, glittering, many-faceted work, then, the critic's (and the reader's) technique must mirror the poet's. Rather than simply studying a selected few of the most famous or difficult poems, we must first survey each section as a whole, savor the over-all impression that Yeats worked so carefully to make on the mind, and then examine the individual links in the chain, picking out the most important ones for special study. In this way we can better appreciate the complex achievement of the whole collection, as well as the simple brilliance of so many of its parts.

THE WANDERINGS OF OISIN

INTRODUCTION: Yeats' first important poem was *The Wanderings of Oisin*, which was originally placed with other narrative and dramatic works in a special section at the back of the *Collected Poems* (where it can still be found in certain editions). But when he revised the book, almost on his deathbed, Yeats restored *Oisin* to its true chronological position at the front of the volume, the beginning of his literary career. Such a placement was wise for several reasons. First, built as it is around Irish mythological subjects and personages, *Oisin* (pronounced *OO-sheen*) sets the tone for much of Yeats' later work, for the poet, as we shall see, was to devote much of his finest poetry—and most of his best plays—to Celtic material. Second, and perhaps even more important, *Oisin* deals with a theme that was to become Yeats'

11

central obsession and most persistent concern—one of the great subjects of poetry, classical as well as romantic—the theme of old age versus perpetual youth, mortality versus immortality,˙ change versus changelessness. Made immortally young by a faery's spell, Oisin, almost despite himself, still longs for his old human surroundings. And then, having lost his eternal youth through a compassionate human impulse, he rages against the sorrows of old age, as Yeats himself was to rage so many years later in so much of his greatest poetry.

> First that sea-rider Oisin led by the nose
> Through three enchanged islands, allegorical dreams,
> Vain gaiety, vain battle, vain repose,
> Themes of the embittered heart . . .
>
> W. B. Yeats, "The Circus Animals' Desertion"

BOOK I.   The poem is in the form of a dialogue between the Fenian hero, Oisin (the son of Finn, the most famous Irish hero of all, from whose name the word *Fenian* is derived, meaning "of the tribe of Finn"), and St. Patrick. The saint listens and occasionally interpolates pious comments as Oisin recounts the tale of his adventures with Niamh, a supernatural (and therefore immortal) maiden who has fallen in love with him. In Book I Oisin tells the saint that he was out hunting with his friends and brothers when "a pearl-pale high-born lady"—Niamh—rode up out of the sea. She explained that she had ridden far from the Danaan land (the legendary land of the faeries) to seek the love of Oisin, for his heroic exploits are known throughout the world. At the sight of her, Oisin falls "into a desperate gulph of love," and when she proposes that he "mount by me and ride/To shores by the wash of the tremulous tide,/Where men have heaped no burial-mounds,/ And the days pass like a wayward tune . . . And the blushes of first love never have flown," he readily agrees. Flying over "the glossy sea" on Niamh's beautiful horse, the couple soon come to the Island of Dancing, a land of eternal youth, where blithe young men and maidens perpetually dance and make merry.

Here, in this country of the young—the immortal young—what Wordsworth called "the still sad music of humanity" is far away; ". . . here there is nor Change nor Death,/But only kind and merry breath,/For joy is God and God is joy . . . And things that have grown sad are wicked." Yet after a hundred unblemished years of perpetual happiness and pleasure Oisin strangely enough wearies of this perfect, irresponsible youth. Chancing upon some old warrior's staff, he is reminded of his own past and his own people, and he weeps, "remembering how the Fenians stept/Along the blood-bedabbled plains,/Equal to good or grievous chance." Then Niamh knows that the time has come for her and her mortal lover to depart, and seek another island. But as they ride away over the sea they can hear behind them the faint sweet song of the ever young:

> An old man stirs the fire to a blaze,
> In the house of a child, of a friend, of a brother.
> He has over-lingered his welcome; the days,
> Grown desolate, whisper and sigh to each other;
> He hears the storm in the chimney above,
> And bends to the fire and shakes with the cold,
> While his heart still dreams of battle and love,
> And the cry of the hounds on the hills of old.

> But we are apart in the grassy places,
> Where care cannot trouble the least of our days,
> Or the softness of youth be gone from our faces,
> Or love's first tenderness die in our gaze.
> The hare grows old as she plays in the sun
> And gazes around her with eyes of brightness;
> Before the swift things that she dreamed of were done
> She limps along in an aged whiteness;
> A storm of birds in the Asian trees
> Like tulips in the air a-winging,
> And the gentle waves of the summer seas,
> That raise their heads and wander singing,
> Must murmur at last, "Unjust, unjust . . .

COMMENT: Yeats' vision here, as thoughout *The Wanderings of Oisin*, is a kind of Blakeian vision of the world, cast symbolically in mythical terms. Thus this land of perpetual youth stands, reasonably enough, for youth itself, the youth through which Oisin, the hero, passes on his life-journey, which is also the journey of the poem. Like the young men and maidens of the Island of Dancing, all young people—even though they are really mortal—imagine themselves immortal, and thus even human youth in a sense confers a kind of immortality on the young—subjective and mistaken, to be sure, but nevertheless real. Yet sooner or later the hero longs to be gone, as most men do. The dream-like perpetual innocence and pleasure of the country of the young is cloying and dissatisfying; it snares and traps the unlucky souls who cannot repudiate it (as Blake, too, saw) like flies in honeyed flypaper. Only those who are truly young—who still imagine themselves immortal (or, like Niamh, actually *are* immortal)—are still happy, though, it is important to note (especially for later reference) the throbbing, singing birds in their trees are "painted." But for him who must leave—Oisin, for instance, like every mortal—the journey is a sad one. He cannot bear to remain, yet as he departs the song-story of the weary old man and the aging hare accompanies him like a fateful warning.

BOOK II: After they leave the Island of Dancing, Niamh and Oisin—with Niamh ominously troubled by "the fall of tears"—journey on till they reach a gloomier and more violent island. There, in a dark, sea-gulfed castle, Oisin frees a soft-eyed maiden and then with the sword of the sea-god, Mannannan, fights ceaselessly with a particularly terrible and skillful demon, an Old-Man-of-the-Sea-like figure who "amid the shades of night . . . changed and ran Through many shapes." First he is an eel, then a roaring fir tree, then "a drowned, dripping body," etc. Having achieved victory, Oisin feasts with Niamh and the maiden, but then is challenged again by the resurgent demon. And thus he lives for a hundred years, fighting and feasting perpetually on this "Island of Victories" until he wearies of this life too, and is ready to move on. "Love, we go/To the Island of Forgetfulness," Niamh murmurs, "for lo!/The Islands of Dancing and of Victories/Are empty of all power." "And which of these/Is the Island of Content?" Oisin asks, to which Naimh can only weepingly reply, "None know."

COMMENT: One interpretation of the Island of Victories (there have been many, as there have been of all these islands) might be that it represents the prime of a man's life, his battle to understand and control the tumultuously shifting reality of life which confronts him, his alternating victories and defeats, his vigorous battles followed by vigorous feasts. This is the apparent center of his life, the meat of it, the prime—"with nor dreams nor fears,/Nor languors nor fatigue: an endless feast,/An endless war." But it too cloys in time, as youth's pleasures cloy—for "light is man's love, and lighter is man's rage;/His purpose drifts and dies." Change is the essence of the mortal soul and the "Island of Content" is what Yeats later called "the sweet far thing," the perfect fulfillment that humanity, almost by definition, can never find.

BOOK III: At last Niamh and Oisin come to the Island of Forgetfulness, a magic land inhabited by huge white creatures, "a monstrous slumbering folk," asleep beneath immense and wrinkled trees. "So long were they sleeping, the owls had builded their nests in their locks,/Filling the fibrous dimness with long generations of eyes." They are beautiful, these sleepers, "yet weary with passions that faded when the sevenfold seas were young." And when Oisin addresses them, their leader responds by putting him, too, to sleep. Thus Niamh and Oisin pass their third century together in dim, forgetful dreams among these huge ancient dreamers. But in his dreams the mortal hero sees his ancestors and all the legendary Fenian kings living again, just as the fitful half-sleep of an old man dozing by the fire conjures up visions of his own finite human past. When he wakes, Oisin knows that it is again the moment to depart, but this time he begs Niamh to let him visit his own mortal kingdom, if only for a day. She agrees, but declares that "if only your shoe/Brush lightly as haymouse earth's pebbles, you will come no more to my side." If Oisin touches anything mortal, in other words, his own mortality will come once more upon him and his unnatural eternal youth, prolonged through Niamh's magic, will crumble and decay. (This is a standard fairy-tale device, as old as Cinderella and as modern as James Hilton's *Shangri-la*.) He leaves and wanders sorrowfully through the sad, wrecked Fenian kingdom of his human life, and finally just as "longing for Niamh," he is about to return to her, he catches sight of two men struggling with a load of sand, and automatically, without thinking, leans down to help them. Immediately his immortal youth flees him, and "my years three hundred fell on me." He is now his true self, "a creeping old man, full of sleep, with the spittle on his beard never dry."

COMMENT: The slumbering giants with owls in their hair so evocatively described—"filling the fibrous dimness with long generations of eyes"—are a fitting enough symbol for the aging spirit, dream- and memory-haunted. Their size is especially interesting: with age, the volume of experience expands and becomes huge, bulky, unwieldy. The past is a great load like a large body, and it wearies a man so that he only wants to forget the monstrous physical fact of the present and retreat into the dreamlike depths of his own memories. Old age, of course, is usually described as shrunken, wizened, fragile. And in realistic human terms it certainly is. But in the Blake-like symbolic terms of this poem the gigantism of the aged sleepers seems suitable. Besides, old as they are, they are still immortals, and in their sleep there is something embryonic and womblike, as though this slumber will renew them; as though they will be reborn out of it, revitalized and refreshed. Perhaps that is the difference between them and Oisin. When his humanity claims him once more, he shrivels; his horizon contracts, and he "creeps" the face of the earth. The sack of sand with which he helps his fellows is another interesting symbol of his mortality, for it is useless and heavy like mortality itself, a burden which he nevertheless feels impelled to share.

CONCLUSION: Despite its often fascinating symbolism, *The Wanderings of Oisin* is not really a wholly successful poem. It is frequently uneven, overwritten, dull. Yet it is interesting nonetheless because of the ways in which it prefigures some of Yeats' most important later preoccupations. Another notable aspect of it is its use of meter: Book I is written in a quick, light, dancing tetrameter, suggestive of youth, Book II in a "mature" iambic pentameter, the "norm" of English verse, and Book III in an extended, overripe hexameter, whose long, drowsy lines seem a distillation of sleepy age. A final point to note about *The Wanderings of Oisin* is the strong Blakeian and Shelleyan influences it shows. Book I sounds particularly Blakeian (like the Blake of the early songs) in lines like "God is joy and joy is God" and of course the symbolism throughout is ultra-Blakeian. The whole concept of this kind of narrative poem, too, is romantic, and the extravagant, romantic, quest-like journey of the hero is especially reminiscent of Shelley (cf. *Alastor* in particular), who, along with Blake, was one of Yeats' earliest and most enduring literary idols.

CROSSWAYS

INTRODUCTION: Yeats often remarked that he would like to forget and even omit from the *Collected Poems* this first book of lyrics, published in 1889, when he was only twenty-four. But then, he wrote (in 1925) "I have . . . remembered an old school friend who has some of them by heart, for no better reason, as I think, than that they remind him of his own youth." And so he did the next best thing; he revised *Crossways* carefully and, as always, superbly. Thus we must remember in reading this section of the *Collected Poems* that many of the poems don't appear in anything like their original form; they are much improved. The mood of this early work remains the same, however. Despite all his revisions Yeats could not edit out (and probably would not want to edit out) the essential spirit of *Crossways*—a lush, shadowy, pre-Raphaelite kind of music infinitely softer, slower and less precise in tone and tempo than the famous stripped violence of his later style.

At the time he wrote these poems Yeats was, first, a schoolboy, just beginning to make himself part of Dublin literary circles, and later, a very young man, just trying to establish himself on the London literary scene. Later—in the 1890's—he was to become a leading figure in London literary circles. As we have noted earlier, he, Lionel Johnson, Ernest Dowson and some others founded the Rhymers' Club in those years and Yeats' work appeared regularly in the *Yellow Book*, the most fashionable periodical of the *fin de siècle*. This early fashionableness of his probably accounts for the slightly derivative, pre-Raphaelite quality of the poems in *Crossways* and some in his next two volumes also. Writers like Yeats and Johnson and Dowson modeled their styles largely on the carefully decorated, ornate, dreamy, art-centered styles of the famous pre-Raphaelites who made up the literary generation immediately preceding theirs— poets like Rossetti and Swinburne, and *litterateurs* like Ruskin and Walter Pater. Indeed, Yeats' own father was—as we have seen—a painter of this school, whose friendships with prominent artists like Burne-Jones and John Morris introduced Yeats from his earliest youth into the most fashionable creative circles. It is no wonder, then, that when he began writing poetry the young Irishman imitated the pre-Raphaelites, blending in, however, just enough of his own admixture of Blake, Shelley, Spenser, and theosophy to make his work a little more distinctive than any-one else's. Certainly he was to become the most successful of the young poets in the Rhymers' Club, though it is often said that if Yeats' style had not undergone so striking a revolution in his middle years, he might never have been anything more than a successful poet in the pre-Raphaelite vein—that is, a successful minor poet.

FIRST POEMS: Even the briefest reading of *Crossways*—simply flipping through the pages—will show how talented, and how derivative, was the young Yeats. The book opens with a pair of pastel pastorals, "The Song of the Happy Shepherd" and "The Sad Shepherd." Yet despite their occasionally "literary" language, their mannered phrases and archaisms, there are some striking and prophetic lines and images in both poems, especially the central assertion of the first that, in a changing and difficult world, "words alone are certain good . . . the wandering earth herself may be/Only a sudden flaming word . . ." As for "The Sad Shepherd," whom "Sorrow named his friend," he is sad because he *cannot* sing as his happy counterpart does. The stars on "their pale thrones" (a persistent image in early Yeats) seem to mock him among themselves, and the wild, indifferent sea by which he walks changes all his sorrowful words "to inarticulate moan." The next poem—"The Cloak, The Boat and the Shoes," also deals with "Sorrow," this time with its paradoxical loveliness, its suddenness and lightness. Following there are a group of

Indian poems—Yeats seems to have gone through an Indian phase at this point, perhaps under the influence of the theosophical and Anglo-Indian literature that was being circulated in Imperial Britain toward the end of the nineteenth century—the most notable being "The Indian to his Love."

"THE INDIAN TO HIS LOVE": Yeats revised this poem considerably in later life, cutting out a number of ponderous and melodramatic abstractions, and as it stands now it is perhaps the most perfect single lyric in *Crossways*. (An extravagant stanza like "There dreary Time lets fall his sickle/And Life the sandals of her fleetness,/And sleek young Joy is no more fickle,/And Love is kindly and deceitless,/And life is over save the murmur and the sweetness," was eliminated entirely, for instance.) The central idea of "The Indian"—reminiscent, perhaps, of Marlowe's famous "Passionate Shepherd," which Yeats may even have been imitating—is simple and clearly stated: the Indian invites his love to live with him in an exotic island paradise where "great boughs drop tranquillity." Here their love will grow like "an Indian star" (lusciously bright, presumably) so that even after they die "our shades will rove/When eve has hushed the feathered ways" (the alleys of the air, where birds fly during the day) "with vapoury" (insubstantial) "footsole by the water's drowsy blaze."

COMMENT: Almost all the images, the adjectives, even the sounds of this poem contribute to the atmosphere of peace and dreamlike quiet that Yeats obviously wanted to construct. The Indian and his love wander "*murmuring* softly lip to lip . . . [ital. mine] how far away are the *unquiet* lands"; they are "hid under *quiet* boughs apart"; their love is "one . . . with the *heavy* boughs . . . the dove that *moans* and *sighs* a hundred days." Even after death their shades "rove" in an evening *hush* by "the water's *drowsy* blaze." But there is one image which is not peaceful and which lifts the poem above the level of a lovely lullaby. At the end of the very first stanza "a parrot sways upon a tree,/Raging at his own image in the enameled sea." This couplet was part of the poem from the beginning and introduces a note of discord into the work, a note of "rage," perhaps, at the Indian's entranced acceptance of his mortality, an acceptance which we did not find, for instance, in Oisin. The poem tells us that this Indian and his love will be peaceful, drowsy, loving ghosts, calm and placid. But in Yeats' later work ghosts are wild and fierce; they rage against their fate. And perhaps the furious parrot here unconsciously prophesied that future fury.

AUTUMNAL MOODS: The next two poems take up the theme

of weariness which was hinted at in the drowsiness of "The Indian to his Love." The opening of "The Falling of the Leaves" is especially evocative. "Autumn is over the long leaves that love us"—an autumn which corresponds to "the waning of love" in the hearts of two sad lovers. And in "Ephemera" "the yellow leaves" fall "like faint meteors in the gloom" as the two lovers part, the lover rather melodramatically assuring his lady that "our souls/Are love, and a continual farewell."

IRISH BALLADS: The next eight poems—the remaining poems in the section—are a group of ballads and songlike lyrics on Irish subjects. Yeats, who was to become *the* great poet of Ireland (though he was actually of Anglo-Irish descent) and a leading figure in the Celtic Revival, was interested in this native folk material from the earliest days of his friendship with John O'Leary. "The Madness of King Goll" deals with an ancient Irish king (of the age of Oisin) who is compelled by madness to wander singing in the wilderness. It is most notable for its evocative, persistent refrain: "They will not hush, the leaves a-flutter round me, the beech leaves old"—Yeats' first use of what was to become a favorite intensifying device throughout his poetic career.

"THE STOLEN CHILD":   Probably the most famous of the early poems in *Crossways*, and the best of the Irish ones, is "The Stolen Child." It is a narrative spoken by the faeries, who tempt a sorrowful human child—as Niamh tempted Oisin—to leave the imperfect world of men for their enchanted (yet somehow sinister) secret places. *"Come away, O human child!"* they insidiously murmur. *"To the waters and the wild/With a faery, hand in hand,/For the world's more full of weeping than you can understand."* And these words become the poem's refrain, whose meaning grows gradually more poignant and frightening as the piece progresses.

In each of the first three stanzas the faery voices describe the wonders of their world—hidden berries, magic dances, enchanted pools where they give the "slumbering trout . . . unquiet dreams"—the same dreams they've given this human child, perhaps. Then in the fourth stanza they triumph—"Away with us he's going,/The solemn-eyed." Yet, as he wends his way toward the waters and the wild, the faeries describe the cosy human world the child has lost— "the calves on the warm hillside . . . the brown mice" bobbing "round and round the oatmeal-chest." Mortality, as Keats knew too, has its own pleasures; he who sacrifices them in search of a magical ideal, often sacrifices the highest good.

COMMENT: This poem is reminiscent of Goethe's *Erl-Konig* (Elf-King), in which the king of the elves appears to a sick child as he rides through the woods with his father and tempts him just as the faeries tempt the stolen child here. But the outcome of Goethe's poem is much more terrifying and dramatic. As the father gallops madly through a mounting storm, trying to get his son to safety, the boy dies in his arms. The fearful and magical figure of the elf-king becomes death itself, a vision of death as it appears to the child in his delirium, death battling with the father for the child's soul. Yeats' poem is much milder; the outcome is vaguer, not so explicit. Yet we, too, sense that "the solemn-eyed" (a complete characterization, in a single phrase, of the sensitive little boy who cannot bear the "weeping" of the world) has made a deadly choice. Amid the cold rush of "the waters and the wild," far from his warm home's hearth, he is the faery's prey. His soul is theirs. The enchantment, the magic that the faeries offer is only another, subtler metaphor for death—death at least to the common joys of humanity.

OTHER POEMS: "To an Isle in the Water" and "Down by the Salley Gardens" are two charming love-songs, the latter written to an exceptionally lovely tune (to be found elsewhere). "The Meditation of the Old Fisherman," another poem of old age, again uses the intensifying device of a simple refrain. The three ballads with which *Crossways* closes tend to be a bit literary and derivative. "Father John" is a rather trivial piece about a good priest; "Moll Magee" the melodramatic story of a mother who inadvertently stifled her baby (by falling asleep on top of it); and "The Foxhunter," the best of the three, yet another narrative about old age. As the aged foxhunter dies, his old "blind hound with a mournful din/Lifts slow his wintry head;/The servants bear the body in;/The hounds wail for the dead"—an effective but again slightly melodramatic last stanza in the grand manner, a stanza which showed, like most of the work in *Crossways*, that the young poet had extraordinary talent which he must still more fully develop and individualize.

THE ROSE

INTRODUCTION: If *Crossways* was a first book of lyrics dealing with Indian and Irish themes in a rather derivative and weary pre-Raphaelite manner, the poems of 1893 which appear in the section later called *The Rose* make more direct use of imagery drawn from a subject which had long been most important to the young poet—the occult. The Irish material, of course, remained central. But Yeats at this point began to blend into it the symbols and concerns of mystical groups like the theosophists, the Dublin hermetic society and the Rosicrucians, to create a tone which was to become most distinctively his, in his early years at least—a tone passionately spiritual, musical, romantic—the voice of an idealistic Irishman.

And yet, though it is helpful to know that Yeats probably drew his central symbol of the rose from the mystical Rosicrucian literature that was being produced in such abundance at the time, the information is not really essential to an understanding of the author's "Rose" poems. One need only recognize that for Yeats, as for many other poets who preceded him—Dante among them—the rose symbolized perfection, a kind of Platonic ideal of immortal beauty and perfection—the shapely spirit which Shelley, in whose footsteps the young poet followed, had called "intellectual beauty." The rose, after all, as D. H. Lawrence (who used the symbol in his poetry too) later remarked, is the chief among flowers, just as the lion is the "king" of beasts. Its perfection is the ecstatic, abstract perfection of shape—fittingly comparable to a Platonic Form. Yet in reality the rose—as poets from Sappho and Horace have lyrically deplored—must die; its perfection is fleeting. Thus when the mortal flower is used to symbolize an immortal ideal—the spirit of beauty—a dimension of poignant irony is added too, arising from the tension between the real and the ideal rose.

Another subject which first appeared in *The Rose* and was later to become centrally important in Yeats' poetry was, of course, his hopeless love for Maud Gonne, the beautiful young Irish actress whom he met in 1889, and whom he was desperately and fruitlessly to woo for the next twenty odd years. Indeed, just as the Rose symbolizes the abstract idea of beauty, Maud Gonne— the beloved to whom so many of Yeats' poems in the next three sections are addressed—comes eventually to symbolize beauty's human embodiment.

"TO THE ROSE UPON THE ROOD OF TIME":   This poem which introduces the section is a passionate invocation of the immortal spirit of beauty, announcing the central theme of the pieces to follow. The poet addresses the "Red Rose, proud Rose, sad Rose of all my days," begging it to be with him while he sings the ancient Irish stories of Cuchulain and Fergus, and the "sad- ness" of eternal beauty that is nevertheless to be found "in all poor foolish things that live a day." Then, in the second stanza he modifies his prayer. "Come near," he begs the immortal Rose, yet not so near that your dazzling perfection can obliterate the weaker claims of "common things." "—Ah, leave me still/A little space for the rose-breath to fill!/Lest I no more hear common things that crave;/The weak worm hiding down in its small cave,/The field-mouse running by me in the grass,/And heavy mortal hopes that toil and pass . . ." Probably Yeats was referring here, among other things, to the attraction esoteric lore had for him; he hoped that he would not lose himself in the winding and obscure byways of the occult, sensing perhaps that much of the strength of his poetry was drawn from the common themes on which he based it (love, age, Ireland, etc.). Finally, he concludes—returning in the last couplet to the substance of the first—"I would . . . sing of the old Eire and the ancient ways;/Red Rose, proud Rose, sad Rose of all my days."

COMMENT: This lovely invocation is easy enough to understand, once one understands the meaning of the Rose symbol and the function of the poem itself as an introduction to the lyrics which are to follow it. Indeed, many of the subjects and poems of this section are actually mentioned in "The Rose upon the Rood of Time"—Cuchulain, Fergus and the Druid, "The Two Trees," "The Rose of the World," "eternal beauty wandering on her way," etc. The point of the second stanza—the poet's desire to still hear "common things"—is reminiscent of "The Stolen Child," who wrongly sacrificed the small common pleasures of life, the brown mice bobbing (here Yeats uses a field-mouse in the same way), for the magic world of the faeries, a symbol of the ideal perhaps comparable to the Platonic Rose. From the first, Yeats, as in *Oisin* too, felt the attraction of both mortality and immortality—though later, in his most famous poems, he was to opt more emphatically for eternity.

The "weak worm" as a specific symbol of mortal, common things, is notably Blakeian; Yeats at this point was working on an ambitious three volume edition of Blake's work, and the weak worm was an image Blake used quite strikingly—and centrally—in "The Book of Thel." The title of the poem, "The Rose Upon the Rood [Cross] of Time," suggests again, quite obviously, the tension between mortality and immortality around which the poem is constructed, and which was, in any case, such a central, persistent concern of Yeats' throughout his life. The eternal Rose, eternal beauty, is yet perceived *in time*—that is, only in mortal things—in a real, mortal rose for instance. Thus the poet asks that he may find "In all poor foolish things that live a day/Eternal beauty wandering on her way."

"OLD EIRE":   The next two poems deal with the promised Irish subjects—Fergus, a great king of ancient Ireland who succumbed to a Druid's enchantment in "a little bag of dreams," and Cuchulain, the legendary Irish hero who was forced through trickery to fight and kill his own son and who then, in madness, rushed down to the shore "and fought with the invulnerable tide." Both subjects will recur again in later volumes. Fergus even appears in this volume, in one of the author's most famous lyrics, "Who Goes with Fergus?" Cuchulain appears in a whole cycle of plays built around the hero's adventures, his life and death, which will be considered in a separate section of this book.

"THE ROSE OF THE WORLD":   "The Rose of the World," the next lyric, is an exquisite, intricately constructed lyric (notice the rhyme scheme, *abbab*, and the way in which the metrical scheme, 55553, enhances it), which deals with the eternity of beauty. "Who dreamed that beauty passes like a dream?" the poet asks, challenging the conventional poetic notion that beauty is fleeting. Not only (stanza 1), he asserts, have men since the Trojans (who died for Helen) died for beauty, but "we and the labouring world are passing by" (stanza 2). That is, beauty endures when *we* do *not*. Furthermore (stanza 3), beauty actually existed *prior* to man: before there were "any hearts to beat" God made the world as "a grassy road" down which eternal beauty might wander.

> **COMMENT:**   This whole poem is like a brilliant geometrical "proof"—musically resonant and sweet—of the statement which the opening question implies: beauty doesn't pass like a dream, men do. (Yeats was, incidentally, quite fond of geometry in his youth—a fondness which was most strikingly manifested in the later *A Vision*, surely the work of a frustrated geometrician turned mystic.) Stanza is linked to stanza, as we saw, with logic and precision, as each elaborates further on the central idea. The informing philosophy, however, is Platonism, for the notion that beauty—or any abstract Form—existed prior to the material world is about as purely Platonic as any notion can be!

MORE ROSES: "The Rose of Peace" and "The Rose of Battle" again make use of the Rose symbol. In the first, beauty brings peace and a kind of Blakeian marriage "of Heaven with Hell;" in the second "The Rose of Beauty" is "the sweet far thing" that calls man on—yet beauty itself is also called on by a "sweet far thing," and has in fact grown sad with its eternity of searching.

SONGS: The next three poems are songs or songlike, "The Faery Song" and "The Cradle Song" equally light and sure in their touch. "The Lake Isle of Innisfree" is one of Yeats' most famous and most widely anthologized poems, though not necessarily one of his best. He was living in London when he wrote it and amid the city grime and bustle felt overcome by nostalgia for the lovely rural Ireland of his childhood. The poem describes the paradisiacal simplicity and tranquility of life on an island in a lake "of Innisfree," where "peace comes dropping slow" (reminding us of the Indians' isle in *Crossways*). The first and third stanzas are the best, with their striking, intense declarations that "I will arise and go now," the vivid descriptions of "the bee-loud glade" and the imaginary "lake water lapping . . . in the deep heart's core."

LOVE: The next four poems deal with love, probably the poet's love for Maud Gonne. The best of them, as they appear in the *Collected Poems* is "The Sorrow of Love," which was much revised by Yeats between the original version and the present one. The intricate beauty and fascination of nature, he declares in the first stanza—"all that famous harmony of leaves," etc.— "had blotted out" man for him, had made him forget humanity, the "common" reality of things with which he had determined in "The Rose Upon The Rood of Time" to concern himself. But then, in stanza two, he recounts how a beautiful girl appeared —Maud Gonne—who "seemed the greatness of the world in tears" (because of her heroic nationalism and political commitment, presumably). As a result of her appearance the poet, in stanza three, asserts that he was returned to the reality of man: nature seemed empty and trivial, the "brilliant moon" became a "climbing moon," the "milky sky" was "empty," the harmonious leaves produced only a "lamentation," all of which reminded the poet only of "man's image and his cry."

DEATH AND FAERIES: "A Dream of Death" and "The Countess Cathleen in Paradise" both deal with the death of beautiful women, who must now sacrifice the body's grace for the soul's. The Countess Cathleen poem was probably inspired by Yeats' work on his play, "The Countess Cathleen," but its opening is striking in itself: "All the heavy days are over"—heavy because fleshly, material, gross, and heavy because hard and difficult—"Leave the body's coloured pride."

"Who Goes With Fergus?"—the famous lyric spoken of earlier (one of its most fascinating appearances is in James Joyce's *Ulysses*, where Stephen Daedalus half mutters it in his drunken stupor in Nighttown) deals with the same Fergus who was tempted by the Druid to abandon his mortal, kingly cares for the enchanted concerns of faeryland. The poem is musical and deliberately vague in the symbolist manner, for Yeats had by now been introduced to the highly influential work of the French *symbolistes* by his close friend Arthur Symons, an authority on the movement. Fergus, who once was a king on earth, now rules the realm of the imagination, and the poet speaks in a faery voice, tempting young men and maids—as the faeries once tempted the stolen child—to "brood on [human] hopes and fear no more," but rather to "pierce the deep wood's woven shade" to where the intricate, shapely enchantment of faeryland is hidden, for powerful Fergus rules "the brazen cars" and all the shadowy dim world of magic which can dispel or perhaps sweeten "love's bitter mystery."

"The Man Who Dreamed of Faeryland" similarly contrasts the ideal and the real, in a poignant story of a man who could never be satisfied with his small triumphs in reality, but wasted his life hungering after the ideal perfection of the faeries. Each stanza describes a different stage in his life, and at each of them his peace is spoiled by the itch for eternity, until at last, even after death, "the man has found no comfort in the grave."

REALITY: The remaining poems deal in various ways with more realistic subjects—the subjects of Irish poetry ("Dedication"), old age, Ireland's future, etc. "The Lamentation of the Old Pensioner" and "The Two Trees" are particularly striking pieces. The first is notable for its bitter words of an old man ("I spit into the face of time/That has transfigured me") and its skillful dramatic variations of the bare refrain ("time/That has transfigured me") pointing toward the stripped yet intricate bitterness of Yeats' *Last Poems.* The second is interesting for its Blakeian use of twin images (comparable to Innocence and Experience): an inner tree which partakes of the spiritual joy and perfection of the ideal world from which the soul should draw its strength, and an evil outer tree which decays like the body in the demonglass of time. One need not know that the two trees are based on esoteric and cabalistic symbols (the tree of life and the tree of knowledge of good and evil) to appreciate this brilliant poem.

THE WIND AMONG THE REEDS

INTRODUCTION: This section (published 1899) represents a kind of early climax for Yeats, a kind of final ripening of his early style. As F. R. Leavis has noted, ". . . with *The Wind Among the Reeds* (1899) the dream-reality takes on a new life, and the poet inhabits it surely. And although the imagery of the Celtic Twilight is heavily worked—'pale,' 'dim,' 'shadowy,' 'desolate,' 'cloud-pale,' 'dream-heavy,'—there is no languor or preciosity here. Indeed, 'passion-dimmed' and 'pale fire' are equally important in the vocabulary. For a new force has entered Mr. Yeats' poetry—love. It is mainly despairing love and the poetry is extremely poignant."

The major themes of *The Wind Among the Reeds* remain the same as those of *Crossways* and *The Rose*—the contrast between mortality and immortality, the ordinary and the beautiful, as represented by humanity and the faeries, or a human object and a rose; the past and future of Ireland; love, and especially Yeats' love for Maud Gonne. Only, as Leavis noted, there is greater emphasis on love. Yeats' passion for Maud Gonne had by now become his central obsession, though, as was shown earlier, he used his beloved (much as he had used the Rose) to symbolize human perfection as a kind of Platonic Form of human beauty. In doing this, Yeats was working, of course, in one of the oldest traditions of poetry, a tradition which dates back to thirteenth-century Florence, to Dante and Cavalcanti, and the Neoplatonists who followed them (and perhaps even further back, to the more idealistic of the twelfth-century Provençal *trouvères*). Poets like those customarily addressed their lyrics to a beloved lady who seemed to embody all that was lovely in the mortal world. Dante, for instance—as everyone knows—consecrated his poems to Beatrice, a Florentine maiden whom he hardly knew, but who symbolized beauty and spiritual perfection for him, much as Maud Gonne symbolized man's nobility and beauty for Yeats. The Neoplatonists held, after Dante, that through such a poetic and idealistic perception of a woman's beauty, a man could more clearly apprehend the beauty of the universe—that is, that her finite earthly beauty would eventually lead him to an appreciation of the infinite spiritual beauty of the divine. Yeats, as we have seen, was influenced by Platonism in all its forms, and his treatment of Maud Gonne in these early poems is certainly one of them.

The prevailing tone of the verses, in keeping with this idealistic conception of the woman to whom they are addressed, is spiritual, with a kind of resonant, dim, abstract music informing the lines. The poet, however, is a healthy, passionate—and frustrated—young man, and cannot wholly restrain his sensuousness. In his later poetry, of course, Yeats often wrote frankly and powerfully of sex and sexual feelings, but at this point his sexuality is only indirectly expressed, in the intensity of the lyrics and especially in his recurrent use of a suggestive sexual symbol like *hair*. Hair is everywhere in these poems—"dim hair," "shadowy hair," "cloudy hair," etc. It reminds us of those pre-Raphaelite paintings of pale, long-faced beauties whose heavy, dark hair, unbound or piled high, was almost their most distinctive feature. Yet, pre-Raphaelite or not, the function of hair in *The Wind Among the Reeds* is clear: it humanizes the unattainable, shadowy beloved of the poet's dreams, and gives sexual force to his longing for her.

"THE HOSTING OF THE SIDHE":   This first poem of the section is one of Yeats' most marvelously evocative lyrics. The poet himself explained in a note who and what the Sidhe were: "The gods of ancient Ireland, the Tuatha de Danaan, or the Tribes of the goddess Dana, or the Sidhe, from Aes Sidhe, or Sluagh Sidhe, the people of the Faery Hills, as the words are usually explained, still ride the country as of old. Sidhe is also Gaelic for wind, and certainly the Sidhe have much to do with the wind. They journey in whirling wind, the winds that were called the dance of the daughters of Herodias in the Middle Ages (Herodias doubtless taking the place of some old goddess). When old country people see the leaves whirling on the road they bless themselves, because they believe the Sidhe to be passing by. Knocknarea is in Sligo, and the country people say that Maeve, still a great queen of the western Sidhe, is buried in [Clooth-na-Bare] the cairn of stones upon it." As the host, the great enchanted and (literally) enchanting company of faeries rides the Irish countryside, they call to mortals with the voice of the calling wind in whose magic folds they whirl. Niamh, the supernatural maiden who bound Oisin in her spell, is among them, and the dream of immortality she and her fellows offer is the same with which she tempted that early hero, and the same, too, with which the faeries had tempted the stolen child and the man who dreamed of faeryland, the temptation of Fergus' kingdom, "the woven shade" of the magic wood and the fabulous journey of the "wandering" stars. Seductive as they are, with "burning hair" tossing in the furious rush of the wind, their words are a warning as well as a temptation; "if any gaze on our rushing band,/We come between him and the deed of his hand,/We come between him and the hope of his heart." He who dreams of faeryland, as we have seen, can never again be satisfied by human life. But then, the poet adds, where in the mortal world "is there hope or deed as fair" as the supernatural beauty of the faeries?

COMMENT: The magic of this poem is almost wholly musical, incantatory. Even more than most of Yeats' melodious early poems this one should be chanted aloud to be really *felt*. The meaning is clear, obvious and familiar to readers of *Oisin*, *Crossways* and *The Rose*. But the sound, the song is incomparable: it is the long, intense, seductive whisper of the wind along an empty country road, a whisper that seems to live in the leaves and call like an invisible voice in the sky, the grass, the sea, the reeds. It is the voice of "the wind among the reeds," the faery-call.

THE POET'S RESPONSE: The next three poems deal with the poet's response to the impossible call of the immortal and the supernatural. "The Everlasting Voices" is a direct response to the faery's temptation in "The Hosting of the Sidhe," the poet impatiently begging the "sweet everlasting Voices" to "be still," for human hearts are too weary to follow them. "The Moods" deals further with this theme of weariness; its tense, stripped lines foreshadow the epigrammatic Yeats of *The Green Helmet* and *Responsibilities*. "The Lover Tells of the Rose in his Heart" substitutes the rose and the beloved (fused in a single symbol) for the faeries as an image of immortality. The common, clumsy, "unshapely things" of humanity, the poet says, "wrong" the perfect "image" of his beloved, the image of immortal perfection, "that blossoms [like] a rose in the deeps of my heart."

IRISH AND FOLK POEMS: Except for "The Fish," which seems to be addressed again to the beloved (or else to the "glimmering" fish-girl of the later "Wandering Aengus"), the next seven poems are all Irish poems, dealing generally with the subject of unattainable perfection within the framework of folk stories or themes. "The Host of the Air" is a particularly charming ballad about a young man whose bride is stolen by the faeries. In a vision he sees her among them "with a sad and a gay face," and afterwards, when he awakens, he hears "high up in the air/A piper piping away,/And never was piping so sad,/And never was piping so gay."

> **COMMENT:**   The ambiguity of O'Driscoll's, and Yeats' feelings toward the faeries is very well illustrated by the simultaneous sadness and gaiety of Bridgit and the pipers. Faeryland is enchanting, magic, desirable; the immortals are gay. But to leave humanity and the comfort of human things is sad; and being immortal, the faeries, too, are weary.

"The Unappeasable Host" is a powerful poem, a kind of lament spoken by a mother, who compares the furious immortality of "the unappeasable host" (the faeries) who will "ride the North" when mortal things have died, with the comfortless, desolate Heaven and Hell of Christianity. "I . . . hear the narrow graves calling my child and me," laments the mother, to whom the Church can only offer death and a questionable afterlife. To her, the immortal and "unappeasable host" seems "comelier than candles at Mother Mary's feet."

COMMENT: This is one of the first appearances of Christianity in Yeats' lyrics, but it is a significant one, for later on such a questioning, such an attempt to come to terms with the Christian legend was to be increasingly interesting to the poet. His play, "The Countess Cathleen," written at about this time, dealt with aspects of Christianity too.

"The Song of Wandering Aengus," another one of Yeats' most famous and widely anthologized early narratives, tells the story of an ancient Irishman, in some legends a kind of god or hero of poetry, who had a vision of a "glimmering" supernatural girl. She becomes the "sweet far thing," like the faeries, that calls him on and on, in the vain, never-to-be-fulfilled hope of plucking, "till time and times are done,/The silver apples of the moon,/The golden apples of the sun"—the impossible fruit of immortality.

"The Song of the Old Mother" and "The Heart of the Woman" are two vividly dramatic lyrics which skillfully delineate both character and situation. They should remind us that Yeats, at this time, was becoming increasingly involved in theatrical work, play-writing out of which both these poems probably grew.

LOVE POEMS: The next seven poems are love poems dealing with the poet's love for Maud Gonne and his relationship with Olivia Shakespear (cf. General Introduction) in the manner described earlier. "He Remembers Forgotten Beauty" is a good example of the kind of idealism with which Yeats treated his beloved. When he holds her in his arms, the poet declares, he holds in his arms all "the loveliness/That has long faded from the world," for she, in her own person, embodies the eternal Platonic Form—and all the "high lonely mysteries"—of "white Beauty."

The strange and lovely ballad of "The Cap and Bells," another widely anthologized lyric, first occurred to Yeats in a dream, as he tells us in a note to the poem. "I dreamed this story exactly as I have written it, and dreamed another long dream after it, trying to make out its meaning, and whether I was to write it in prose or verse. . . . The poem has always meant a great deal to me, though, as is the way with symbolic poems, it has not always meant quite the same thing. Blake would have said, 'The authors are in eternity,' and I am quite sure they can only be questioned in dreams." But though Yeats felt the poem could not really be explained, it is easy to understand at least something of it. It is rather plainly a poem about poetry, about the way in which, when Yeats, the lover, failed to win his beloved with all his ordinary human efforts—his heart and soul—he finally managed to gain her attention through the means of his art, his "cap and bells," which at last obtained a hearing for his heart and soul.

LOVE AND THE ROSE: The next six poems are again all love poems, with the exception of "The Valley of the Black Pig," which deals with an Irish legend about the end of the world and is addressed to the "master of the still stars and of the flaming door," the Lord of the Universe who will alone survive.

Then "The Blessed" and "The Secret Rose" both return to the "Incorruptible Rose," the "Far-off, most secret, and inviolable Rose," as a symbol of immortality. But again, in "He Wishes for the Cloths of Heaven," "The Lover Pleads with His Friends," etc., Yeats builds his poems around his love for Maud Gonne. At last, in "He Thinks of His Past Greatness When a Part of the Constellations of Heaven," Yeats reaches a precision of bitter and passionate statement in dealing with this subject that he had not achieved before. Though the poem is based on the oriental doctrine of Karma, of reincarnation, with the poet asserting that through a magic spell he knows the secrets of his past, its central thought is that now, having become "a man, a hater of the wind" (of the faery voices that lure mortals on), the poet must confront the terrible truth of the hopelessness of his love—"that his head/ May not lie on the breast, nor his lips on the hair/Of the woman that he loves until he dies." The directness, the frank sexual frustration, give force here, where the dim, dream-clogged imagery of some of the other poems had tended merely to evaporate into thin air. The last two lines are intense, overwhelming: "O beast of the wilderness, bird of the air,/Must I endure your amorous cries?" The melodious boy, remade by passion and despair, is moving toward a sparer and bitterer new style.

"THE FIDDLER OF DOONEY":   This light and delightful little ballad, which closes the book, clears away the bitterness of "He Thinks of His Past Greatness," and ends things on a wonderful, merry note. But it is a meaningful note, too: the fiddler's brother and cousin are conventional, religious men, but the fiddler's own religion is his art, his gay fiddling. And it is this gaiety, this merriment, which will get him into heaven ahead of his pious relatives—for St. Peter knows that "the good are always the merry,/. . . And the merry love to dance."

> And when the folk there spy me,
> They will all come up to me,
> With 'Here is the fiddler of Dooney!'
> And dance like a wave of the sea.

It is Yeats the fiddler, not the disappointed lover, who speaks to us here, the jester who hoped to win his lady with his cap and bells, the gay singer of Ireland, whose singing will persist like a wave of the immortal sea, despite all mortal setbacks.

IN THE SEVEN WOODS

INTRODUCTION: Between *The Wind Among the Reeds* and this briefer volume of 1904 two important things happened to Yeats. First, he became seriously involved in theatrical business (he'd confined himself simply to play-writing before), founding with his patroness, Lady Gregory, Edward Martyn and George Moore the Irish theatre society which ultimately became the world-famous Abbey Theatre. And second, he experienced, in February 1903, the terrible shock of Maud Gonne's marriage to Major John MacBride. The impact of this news was overwhelming. Indeed, except for lyrics for plays and a scattering of verses which, as it were, forced themselves out here and there, Yeats wrote hardly any personal lyric poetry for seven years afterward, between 1903 and 1910.

Yet the whole experience of these years, because of the striking change in Yeats' poetic manner which they produced, was perhaps even more valuable than any lyrics the poet might have written in the period. The stylistic necessities of play-writing—conversational exactness, dramatic bareness, the kind of sustained verbal tension and sinewy style which could easily communicate a mood or an emotion to an audience—began to strip his poetry of some of its baroque dreaminess. The anguish of what seemed a final rejection by Maud Gonne, to whom he had dedicated so much love and so many verses, helped the process along. Bitter, despairing, disillusioned, Yeats seemed suddenly to awake from the long, idealistic dream of his youth, and by the time he wrote *The Green Helmet* he was more completely involved with the workaday world around him than he ever had been before. *In The Seven Woods* is a transition volume, the work of a sleeper slowly waking, a disillusioned lover who cannot yet bring himself to plunge, for forgetfulness, into the common bustle of reality.

"IN THE SEVEN WOODS":   The phrase "In the Seven Woods," which serves as title for both the book and this introductory poem, refers to the Seven Woods of Lady Gregory's estate, where Yeats wrote many of these lyrics. This particular one is a rather cool, detached, conversational poem in the new manner, which seems to have been written chiefly to praise the soothing, quiet and aristocratic calm of Lady Gregory's domain. Like many poets of the past who dutifully wrote carefully crafted verses to praise their noble patrons, Yeats produced a good number of skillful verses in honor of Augusta Gregory, the wealthy Irish aristocrat (herself a famous playwright) who for 20 years provided him with beautiful summer surroundings (her home at Coole Park) along with devoted friendship and warm encouragement. The difference is that Yeats' feelings for his patroness were not dutiful but intensely sincere: he valued Lady Gregory's friendship perhaps more highly than any other he had, and he was a man passionately devoted to his friends.

The basic statement of "In the Seven Woods" is simple and rather clear. In the calm of Lady Gregory's estate, the poet says, where the pigeons "make their faint thunder" (a wonderful phrase for the rumbly, alto murmur of a flock of pigeons in the trees!) the poet has been able to forget all "the old bitterness" that empties the heart—not only the private bitterness of his failure with Maud Gonne, but also the public bitterness of Ireland's subservience to the "new commonness" of another English king (Edward VII). For in these woods "Quiet" still "wanders laughing and eating her wild heart," and the "Great Archer" of the skies, "who but awaits His hour to shoot, still hangs/A cloudy quiver over Pairc-na-lee"—that is, he still withholds his terrible arrows.

> **COMMENT:**   The last four lines are the most difficult of the poem, for they provide it with a basic ambiguity—an "ironic undercutting," in John Unterecker's words, of the poet's professed "contentment." Though Quiet wanders the woods laughing, she is also "eating her wild heart"—eating her heart out, that is, with a secret—a concealed grief, a grief that Yeats presumably shares. And the arrow which the archer withholds must yet, the poet knows, sooner or later be shot. This last image, incidentally, is a fine indefinable image in the symbolist manner. While the Archer may be, in literal terms, Sagittarius, the constellated archer of the skies, he is obviously something more, too. His "cloudy quiver" suggests not the night of glittering Sagittarius but a sultry daytime, a gloomy afternoon. Death? Pain? Grief? Unrequited love? The Knowledge of Good and Evil? He is all of these, and his arrows are the arrows of pain and self-knowledge, the arrows of Blakeian Experience.

ARROWS: The next five poems are all such arrows of pain, dealing with one or another aspect of Yeats' painful love for Maud Gonne. The first, "The Arrow," expresses his regret at her gradual aging. Years have passed since the young poet and the girl with the "apple-blossom" skin first met (Maud Gonne was standing near a bowl of apple blossoms at their first meeting, Yeats later related, and he ever after associated her beauty with that flower) and now the middle-aged poet grieves that "no man may look upon" his beloved any more as she was then, in the first flush of her beauty. "The Folly of Being Comforted" seems to reply to "The Arrow." Though Maud Gonne is not the delicate, youthful beauty that she was, the years have but added further to "that great nobleness of hers." In fact, "time can but make her beauty over again," and the poet's heart knows it cannot be comforted by the thought that her looks are gone.

"Old Memory" and "Never Give All the Heart" deal more specifically with the bitterness of the poet's loss, while "The Withering of the Boughs" deals with his loss symbolically. "The boughs" that "have withered because I have told them my dreams" are the boughs of the tree of his life, his youth, which have withered because he poured all the strength of his dreams into his love (and his poems) for Maud Gonne.

"ADAM'S CURSE":   This poem is often regarded as a pivotal one in Yeats' stylistic development. Not only does it perfectly illustrate his "new" conversational manner, but it actually expounds the new theory of poetry on which that manner is based. "A line [of poetry] will take us hours maybe," the poet tells Maud Gonne and her sisten Kathleen (for they were the originals of the beautiful women of the poem) "yet if it does not seem a moment's thought,/Our stitching and unstitching has been naught"—that is, a poet's labor should be to seem spontaneous, his effort to appear effortless. Yet, simple as a poem may seem, "to articulate sweet sounds together," the poet adds, is harder work than any other. To which the "beautiful mild woman," Maud Gonne's sister, replies that women know very well that one "must labour to be beautiful." Indeed, the poet responds in *his* turn, there have also been lovers (in the Middle Ages, for instance) who thought *love* should be worked at too: "They would sigh and quote with learned looks/Precedents out of beautiful old books;/Yet now it seems an idle trade enough."

At this all three fall silent, as the weary shell of a moon climbs "the trembling blue-green of the sky." And Yeats thinks reproachfully—a thought for Maud Gonne's ears alone—that he too had tried to love "in the old high way," and "it had all seemed happy, and yet we'd grown/As weary-hearted as that hollow moon."

> **COMMENT:**   Though the pastel weariness of the poem's ending—the shell-like, time-wasted moon and blue-green sky—suggest Yeats' dreamy and weary early style, "Adam's

Curse" illustrates his new manner in several important ways. First of all, it is a dialogue, which, seemingly casual and effortless, expounds the poet's theories of effortlessness in a conversational style to which his play-writing had accustomed him. As John Unterecker has noted, this sort of dramatized conversation was to become one of Yeats' "most characteristic form[s]," though often the dialogue in later poems is inner, rather than outer. But besides its easy conversational manner, "Adam's Curse" is put together more casually, less symmetrically, than most of the elegantly balanced lyrics the poet had written heretofore. The stanzas are all of different—unequal—lengths, and there are a number of half-rhymes, both assonances and dissonances (clergymen/thereupon; enough/love; strove/love; grown/moon). The careful logic and precision with which the poet advances from point to point in making his central statement is familiar, however. Compare, for instance, the progression here from poetic labour to beauty's labour to love's labour (a subtle evolution of a theory of art into a theory of life) with the similarly careful logic of the earlier "The Rose of the World." It is still the same Yeats we have to deal with, but one whose powers are ripening and expanding rapidly.

SONGS AND BALLADS: With a few exceptions the remaining poems in this section are songs and ballads, many from plays. "Red Hanrahan's Song About Ireland" is a kind of nationalistic piece in praise of Cathleen ni Houlihan, the legendary Irish heroine about whom Yeats also wrote a famous play. "The Ragged Wood," with its passionate outburst—"O my share of the world, O yellow hair!"—and "O Do Not Love Too Long," are almost desperately intense love songs. "The Old Men Admiring Themselves in the Water," "Under the Moon," and "The Players Ask for a Blessing" are all equally bitter. "All that's beautiful drifts away/Like the water," mutter the old men, while the poet mourns, in "Under the Moon," that to dream of beautiful women "is a burden not to be borne," and the players grieve that while "the proud and careless notes" of the play "live on," "our hands, our hands, must ebb away." The last poem, "The Song of the Happy Townland," is a wonderful ballad about a place where things do *not* ebb away: an immortal townland, a kind of peasant Paradise, where "Rivers are running over/With red beer and brown beer," and swords and trumpets hang on the gold and silver boughs beneath which "Queens, their eyes blue like the ice,/ Are dancing in a crowd." Though the poet's style was changing, his central obsession remained the same—disappointed, defeated in love, he still sought an image of eternity which he might oppose to the ebb and flux of mortal things. The Rose and the beloved might desert him, but like the rider to the happy townland he would ride on, seeking new symbols in a prophetically "golden and silver wood."

THE GREEN HELMET

INTRODUCTION: *The Green Helmet* continues in the mood and manner of *In the Seven Woods*. Like the earlier volume, it deals mostly with the pain of what the poet was later to call his "barren passion" for Maud Gonne, but his style has now evolved even further into a kind of stripped precision of bitterness, as though the fever of rejected love had dried up all that earlier dreamy lushness, leaving only the bones of poetry. Thus most of the verses have short, terse, sinewy lines—tensely and intensely conversational—probably more a result of Yeats' play-writing than of his passion.

Play-writing and "theatrical business," too, had brought the poet by now into the kind of constant regular association with the workaday world that would wear away anyone's dreaminess, especially a sensitive poet's. Therefore the poems in this volume that don't deal with disappointed love are political or epigrammatic observations, fierce or cynical public pronouncements of a sort Yeats had not made before this, but which would become increasingly familiar to his readers as his public career advanced. *The Green Helmet* (cf. section on Yeats' "Cuchulain Plays") is also the title of a play Yeats wrote at this time, in which the helmet belongs to a famous warrior, the Red Man, whose challenge Cuchulain heroically accepts. It is a challenge Yeats accepts too—the challenge of unswerving loyalty to a tumultuous and corrupt Ireland, "this country that was made when the devil spat."

MAUD GONNE AGAIN: After the introductory "His Dream" —a kind of dramatized meditation on the dignity of death (which, after all, is only another form of eternity), all the poems through "Against Unworthy Praise" are about Maud Gonne. "A Woman Homer Sung," "No Second Troy" and "Peace" deal with her in Homeric terms, comparing her with the noble women—especially Helen, and perhaps Athena—about whom Homer wrote in *The Iliad*. Hers is a "beauty like a tightened bow, a kind/That is not natural in an age like this" ("No Second Troy"). And the tension of such beauty drove her to occasional political excesses. Among the dull, workaday, middle-classes of modern Ireland, in other words, what could a keeper of the ancient flame of heroism like Maud Gonne have done but become excessive? "Why, what could she, have done, being what she is?/Was there another Troy for her to burn?"

COMMENT: This Homeric, and specifically Trojan, imagery has appeared in Yeats' poems before (cf. "The Rose of the World"—"For these red lips, with all their mournful pride . . . Troy passed away in one high funeral gleam") but it is to become increasingly important in his work. Troy itself came to seem to Yeats an historical point of great significance, an intersection of two civilizations where mounting mutual tensions exploded into a final conflagration after which one sank into oblivion and the other went on to international ascendency. Helen, the beautiful woman who triggered the war, and Leda, her mother, were central figures, of course, whose actions determined Troy's fate—and the world's. They hold an endless fascination for Yeats who, gentle and dreamy himself, always longed to learn the secret of power, the secret of those rare and magical individuals who, through beauty, nobility or bravery, can command the respect and influence the lives of their fellowmen. It was a secret, Yeats thought, known as instinctively by "the women Homer sung" as by a man like Cuchulain, Ireland's own ancient hero.

"Reconciliation," another of the Maud Gonne poems, was written after the actress' marriage to Major MacBride ended in estrangement in 1905. The poet was, of course, overjoyed when Madame MacBride (as she was frequently called) asked him to handle some of the details of the separation. "Against Unworthy Praise" resolves, finally the ambiguous doubts and hopes with which Yeats approaches both his love for Maud Gonne and his desire for public praise. It doesn't matter to him, he declares (in lines addressed to his own heart), whether or not people in general like his work, for it has all been written for his beloved, has been "a secret between" the two of them, "between the proud and the proud." Yet if his heart "still longs for praise," Yeats declares, it should turn to "a haughtier text"—"the labyrinth of [Maud Gonne's] days/That her own strangeness perplexed"—that is, the complexity and bitterness of her life, caused by her extravagant actions (cf. "No Second Troy")."Yet she, singing upon her road," the poet exclaims, in admiration and surprise, "Half lion, half child [thus almost a kind of sphinx-like figure] is at peace."

"THE FASCINATION OF WHAT'S DIFFICULT":   This brief, lean, angry poem perhaps most powerfully expresses Yeats' *Green Helmet* mood. "The Fascination of What's Difficult," he declares, has absorbed his peace and embittered his life. But this still does not seem right to him, for though he'd commented in "Adam's Curse" that "to articulate sweet sounds together" requires terrible labour, he can't help thinking "there's something ails our colt" (Pegasus, the flying horse of poetry) if it must "strain, sweat and jolt" as if "it had not holy blood," instead of sailing smoothly through the air. The poem closes, succinctly, with the poet's "curse on plays/That have to be set up in fifty ways . . . Theatre business, management of men," the petty details of which are so exasperating that "I swear before the dawn comes round again/ I'll find the stable and pull out the bolt," so that the holy horse, the spirit of poetry, can escape completely!

> **COMMENT:**   This is one of Yeats' first epigrammatic public pronouncements, and it was obviously prompted by the mundane complexities of his association with the Abbey Theatre. Yet despite the apparent bitterness of his half-humorous denunciation of "theatre business, management of men" (a denunciation which is cast, incidentally, in a brilliant conceit), we should not overlook the affirmativeness of the title—the *fascination* of what's difficult. Though the poet toys with the idea of giving the whole thing up, he is really fascinated by the difficult challenge of this new reality which he, the one-time dreamer, has set out to conquer. And in keeping with this fascination, many of his future poems will be devoted to realistic concerns, taking various stands, both vehement and witty, on all the most difficult issues of public life.

EPIGRAMS AND ASSERTIONS: "A Drinking Song," "The Coming of Wisdom with Time," "On Hearing that the Students of Our New University Have Joined the Agitation Against Immoral Literature," and "To A Poet Who Would Have Me Praise Certain Bad Poets, Imitators of His and Mine," are all lean, witty, epigrammatic little verses, illustrating Yeats' mood: "Through all the lying days of my youth," the poet announces, "I swayed my leaves and flowers in the sun;/Now I may wither into the truth." "The Mask," also terse and epigrammatic, is based on an idea that was to become one of Yeats' central theories: every man should assume "the mask" of his opposite; style, not sincerity, strikes sparks of interest among men. In other words, Yeats recognized, as most people do, that we all have "public" personalities, public faces that we put on to impress others. A shy man, like Yeats himself, may hide his shyness behind a mask of boldness, and this, the poet declared, elevating an observation into a doctrine, is all to the good. Such deliberate drama enriches and illuminates life, providing the metaphors and the "fire" out of which poetry, as well as passion, must grow.

"Upon a House Shaken by the Land Agitation" and "At Galway

Races" are both important political utterances which show Yeats moving to a seriously conservative, aristocratic position. Though the poet was not actively anti-democratic, he felt—as many other contemporary poets have (including T. S. Eliot and D. H. Lawrence)—that the dull, leveling effect of majority rule was bad for art, if nothing else, for art flourishes best in an aristocratic society where it can be nurtured in elegance and ease (as well as by wealthy patrons). Thus "Upon a House" is written about Lady Gregory's estate, which was slated to be taken over by the government in an attempt at more equitable distribution of the land. The poet asks if the world will actually be "luckier" without aristocrats and the tradition of aristocracy to order things with "passion and precision" and finally to produce "a written speech/ Wrought of high laughter, loveliness and ease?" Similarly, in "At Galway Races," he deplores the dullness of a society ruled by "the merchant and the clerk" and hopes that someday the world will be renewed by wild, vivid men of the old aristocratic sort, "men/That ride upon horses."

COMMENT: Houses, as in the first of these poems, and horsemen, as in the second, are two increasingly important images to Yeats. Aristocratic houses, which have stood for centuries on their beautifully ordered estates, symbolize all the best traditions of a hierarchical society, as well as all the grace and substance of the past. Horsemen stand, of course, for aristocrats, since in most cases only wealthy men can afford good riding horses and since horse racing, specifically, was originally an aristocratic sport. Horsemen, even more importantly, must be men of strength, courage and determination in order to control and direct the brute strength of the animals they ride, and so their wild vigor is opposed to "the timid breath" of the middle class "merchant and the clerk."

POETRY AND LOVE: The last two poems in the section compare Yeats' youth and his new maturity while dealing with two of his favorite topics, poetry and love. In "All Things Can Tempt Me" the poet tells us that in his youth love and politics tempted him from poetry, though now it comes quite readily to him. But when he was young he at least believed a poet should sing with a splendid air. Now, however, he only wishes to be "colder and dumber and deafer than a fish," for though the verses come easily enough, he no longer has the heart for them. Still, in "Brown Penny" Yeats re-assumes at least a mask of cheerfulness. He relates how love came to him as carelessly as through the flip of a coin, and how, now that he has loved, he knows that "love is the crooked [puzzling] thing,/There is nobody wise enough/To

find out all that is in it." Yet he accepts his fate philosophically—
"I am looped in the loops of her hair"—and even eagerly—"One
cannot begin it too soon." This lightness and cheerfulness following the numb despair of "All Things Can Tempt Me" reminds us
of the closing of *The Wind Among the Reeds*, where the merry
"Fiddler of Dooney" seemed to clear away all the bitterness of
"He Remembers His Past Greatness." Perhaps Yeats sees himself
as the gay fiddler still—certainly he was working toward a theory
that supernatural gaiety must inform the noblest tragedies
("Hamlet and Lear are gay")—and here, though dejected over his
failure with Maud Gonne, he had already begun to put on the
bravely painted mask of his opposite.

RESPONSIBILITIES

INTRODUCTION: In the ten years between 1910 and 1920
which encompass *Responsibilities*, 1914, and *The Wild Swans at
Coole*, 1919, Yeats, who had been a brilliant but still minor poet,
became a great poet, *the* major poet of at least the first half of
our century. "Withering into truth," as he had intended them to,
his now stark, spare and passionate lines were infused in these
years with a new metaphysical intensity. The fanciful symbols of
faery and Rose forgotten, the poet had yet been unable to abandon
his central concern with what John Unterecker calls "the anguish of
mortality," nor had he been able to relinquish his occult interests,
which stemmed, after all, at least in part from his poetic obsession
with mortality. By the time he was writing the poems of *Michael
Robartes and the Dancer*, *The Tower* and *The Winding Stair*,
probably his three greatest volumes, Yeats, as we shall see, was
devoting much of his energy to meditative and speculative verse
based on such metaphysical concerns. Here, however, in *Responsibilities*, he is still in a transition phase, still playing a vehemently
active political role, hurling epigrammatic abuse at his enemies,
defending Lady Gregory from various attacks, and brooding on
Maud Gonne. But the beginnings of his newly intense metaphysical interest can be clearly seen in brilliant poems like "The
Cold Heaven" and "The Magi," which crown the section.

An important influence on Yeats' style in these years was the
young American poet Ezra Pound, whom he first met in 1909
and who quickly became a close friend (eventually his secretary)
and literary adviser. Though Yeats deplored Pound's over-experi-
mentalism in his own work, he valued his shrewd critical judgments and in many cases followed the younger man's suggestions
that he strip his poetry even further of the ornate imagery with
which it was originally loaded. It was at this time, under the

influence of such ideas (and of a good deal of Japanese and Chinese poetry he read with Pound, including the famous "Fenelossa manuscript" that Pound was then editing) that Yeats began the process of revising—cutting, simplifying and intensifying— all his earlier work that was to go on as long as he lived.

Responsibilities, as Unterecker has perceptively pointed out, is organized along very clear and logical lines, carefully building to the climactic metaphysical poems of "The Magi" and "The Cold Heaven" which indicated the new road the poet was to travel in the future. Working from the title, Unterecker notes, "we can see Yeats' plan for the group as a whole:

> Responsibilities of the poet 'close on forty-nine'
> Supernatural responsibilities
>   Dead ancestors: 'Pardon, Old Fathers'
>   Dead friends who had been poets: 'The Grey Rock'
> Social responsibilities
>   Lane-pictures poems
>   *Playboy*-riots poems
> The function of irresponsibility
>   'Beggarman' poems
> Personal responsibilities
>   Iseult Gonne poems
>   Maud Gonne poems
>   'Friends'
> Aesthetic responsibilities
>   Supernatural models: 'The Magi,' 'The Dolls'
>   Style: 'A Coat'
>   Rededication: 'While I, from that reed-throated whisperer' "

THE QUICK AND THE DEAD: Yeats' supernatural responsibilities—his responsibilities to ghosts, to the dead—are, first, to his ancestors, whom he addresses in "Pardon, old fathers" and second, to his old friends, many of whom—notably the members of the Rhymers' Club, the "companions of the Cheshire Cheese" to whom "The Grey Rock" is directed—are also dead. In the first poem he begs his ancestors to forgive him because "for a barren passion's sake" (his love for Maud Gonne, which kept him from marrying anyone else) "Although I have come close on forty-nine,/I have no child, I have nothing but a book,/Nothing but that to prove your blood and mine." In the second he tells the ghosts of his old friends a story of the old gods of Ireland, and of how they consoled a woman who mourned the death of her lover by drenching her in their immortal wine (comparable to poetry, perhaps), which brought her forgetfulness and laughter.

COMMENT: Yeats' undisguised use of ancestors and dead friends in these two poems is significant for the direction of his future work. As he grew older, his poetry became increasingly frank in its substitution of real people and experiences for the mythological and imaginary subjects about which he'd written earlier. All this is part of his persisting tendency towards greater realism, less dreaminess, and part, too, of his gradually strengthening certainty that poetry is a process of intricate self-dramatization, an escape not *from* but *into* life.

POLITICAL RESPONSIBILITIES: A number of Yeats' poems at this time were inspired by the so-called Lane pictures controversy. Lady Gregory's nephew, Hugh Lane, was an art dealer who had put together an excellent collection of modern French paintings in the course of his career. But when he insisted that a suitable gallery be built to house the pictures—and favored a design by an Englishman!—the Irish nationalists were indignant. "Gradually," as Unterecker puts it, "their attacks extended to Lane and ultimately to the paintings themselves. By 1913 all parties concerned had lost their tempers." Lane wanted money for the gallery raised at once, by private subscription if necessary, for the city of Dublin would only foot a fraction of the bill. But some wealthy men, who could afford to subscribe—like Lord Ardilaun, to whom Yeats' "To A Wealthy Man Who Promised a Second Subscription to the Dublin Municipal Gallery if it were Proved the People Wanted Pictures" is addressed—refused to do so unless the "people," whom Yeats contemptuously characterizes as "Biddy" and "Paudeen," manifested *their* support by chipping in too. Yeats' position in all this was, of course, the aristocratic one. The grand dukes of Urbino and Ferrara, he declares in "To a Wealthy Man," all the noble patrons of the past, supported art because *they* knew it was worthwhile, without consulting the wishes of the mob. "Let Paudeens play at pitch and toss"—let the peasants amuse themselves with their vulgar pursuits, Yeats tells Lord Ardilaun and all aristocrats everywhere: it is the job of a nobleman to set a pattern of nobility for the clumsy herd.

"September 1913," "To a Friend Whose Work Has Come to Nothing," and "To a Shade," (which is addressed to the ghost of the Irish leader, Parnell), deal with the same theme of the mob-majority's commonness, dullness and vulgarity (a theme also treated, as we have seen, in "At Galway Races" and "On a House Shaken by the Land Agitation"). But "Paudeen" significantly modifies Yeats' increasingly arrogant, anti-democratic statements. "Indignant" at the spite and stupidity of old shopkeeper

Paudeen—the symbol of the lower and middle-class majority—
Yeats stumbles through the dawn until suddenly, in the "luminous
wind," amid sweet bird cries, he has a kind of Joycean epiphany:
". . . on the lonely height," he realizes, "where all are in God's
eye,/There cannot be, confusion of our sound forgot,/A single
soul that lacks a sweet crystalline cry." In the eye of God, that is,
far from the clash and clamor of mortal politics, *all* souls, even the
soul of the now vulgar Paudeen, are equal; all speak to God with
the sweet and ringing clarity of birds.

In "On Those that Hated *the Playboy of the Western World*,"
however, a brief but powerful epigrammatic stanza, Yeats returns
to his customary scathing contempt for the masses. The mobs
who rioted at the first performance of Synge's play (they objected
to the play's "immorality") are compared to eunuchs in Hell,
who stare enviously at the strength and potency of Don Juan's
"sinewy thigh."

COMMENT: Brief as it is, this little poem is a memorable
one, with its striking image of the flabby eunuchs railing and
sweating with rage and envy as they stare at the muscular
Juan, who is an embodiment of sexuality directly antithetical to their complete impotence. For Yeats, the legendary lover symbolized "all creative power," just as the lower
middle-class Puritans who hated *The Playboy* symbolized
all cultural "deprivation." But the fact that he cast his
ideas in such frank and forceful sexual terms is a further
manifestation of his new realism. As he grew older, his use
of sexuality became increasingly direct and straightforward,
no longer allusively presented in references to "shadowy
hair," but openly stated in images of Juan's "sinewy thigh"
or the "devil that is between my thighs" ("Beggar to
Beggar").

BEGGAR BALLADS: As Unterecker's plan indicated, Yeats'
beggar ballads perform a "function of irresponsibility"—that is,
they remind the poet and his audience that as an artist he has a
responsibility to be irresponsible sometimes too, not always to be
grave and righteous, a "smiling public man," but to speak up for
the drunkards and beggars, the gay singers and wandering
fiddlers, who, because unburdened of possessions and the cares
possessions bring, see—and speak—the world most truly as it is.
"Running to Paradise" is perhaps the best and most representative of these. Its speaker is a beggar who, as he hurries along the
windy road, compares his careless freedom to the fatigue of his
brother Marteen, "worn out" by the children and servants and
possessions with which he must struggle as a respectable member

of society. "I am running to Paradise," the merry beggar sings, "and there the king is but as the beggar"—his titles, possessions and responsibilities counting for nothing—just as in the eye of God, in "Paudeen," all souls speak with the same sweet crystalline cries.

THE SPECULATIVE IMAGINATION: "What proud death may bring"—the speculative imagination which more and more was to characterize Yeats' work fastened on this subject and on the corollary subject of the relationship between soul and body and began passionately to explore it in a series of poems beginning here with "The Cold Heaven" and ending only at Yeats' death with "The Black Tower," his last lyric. In "The Cold Heaven" the poet's vision of "the cold and rook-delighting heaven/That seemed as though ice burned and was but the more ice"—a sky paradoxically burning with light yet coldly blue—drives his "imagination and heart" wild with old memories of "the hot blood of youth, of love crossed long ago," of the hopeless passion for Maud Gonne on which he has spent so much of his life energy. "Riddled with light" (both *shot through* with a mystical light of understanding and *puzzled* by the inexplicable light of heaven) he cries and trembles and rocks to and fro in despair, then asks a crucial question:

> . . . Ah! When the ghost begins to quicken,
> Confusion of the death-bed over, is it sent
> Out naked on the roads, as the books say, and stricken
> By the injustice of the skies for punishment?

That is, when the new life of the ghost begins (its "life" after death), does it roam the world "naked" and stricken by an eternal injustice comparable to life's injustice—the injustice, say, of Maud Gonne's not returning Yeats' passion, as punishment of its earthly sins—sins precisely like the sin of loving Maud Gonne too much?

Perhaps even more than "The Cold Heaven," "The Magi" indicates the future course Yeats' speculative imagination was to take, for while "The Cold Heaven" presents the poet's metaphysical speculations about life and death in wholly personal terms (which, of course, do lead to a large and impersonal question), "The Magi" objectifies his ideas in the controlled, entirely impersonal image of the travelling wise men—nominally the Magi of Bethlehem but perhaps also their ancestors or descendants, the questing scholars of all ages who have always sought life's ultimate answers. "Unsatisfied" by the "turbulence" of the crucifixion at Calvary—which presented more problems than it solved—these wise men seek "the uncontrollable mystery on the bestial floor"—that is, the source and secret of life itself. And the intensity of their search reminds us of Yeats' own esoteric researches, studies which were soon to produce a system in which Bethlehem and all it represented would play an essential part.

PASSING TIME: Almost every one of Yeats' volumes contains a group of poems on the subject of passing time and how it has affected the poet's dreams, his verses, and his beloved Maud Gonne. Here, in "Responsibilities," "The Witch" and "The Peacock" are two succinct observations on ambition, worldly or unworldly, and its fate in time. "To a Child Dancing in the Wind," and "Two Years Later" are addressed to Iseult Gonne, Maud Gonne's adopted daughter, and compare her innocent and hopeful youth with the poet's experienced—and disillusioned—maturity. "The Memory of Youth" and "Fallen Majesty" express Yeats' poignant recollections of Maud Gonne's one-time beauty "that seemed a burning cloud." "Friends" adds Lady Gregory and Olivia Shakespeare to Maud Gonne in forming a list of the "three women that have wrought/What joy is in my days." And "That the Night Come" deals with the superb "storm and strife" of an uncommon woman's—Maud Gonne's, no doubt—life, a life lived with such passion, such intolerance for "the common good" of things, that it seemed directed only toward "what proud death may bring."

THE NEW AESTHETIC: Succinct and forceful, "A Coat," the next to last poem in the volume, deals again with Yeats in his character of Irish musician—"The Fiddler of Dooney," the singer of "The Brown Penny"—and with the new aesthetic that informs his work from here on.

> I made my song a coat
> Covered with embroideries
> Out of old mythologies
> From heel to throat;
> But the fools caught it,
> Wore it in the world's eyes
> As though they'd wrought it.
> Song, let them take it,
> For there's more enterprise
> In walking naked.

In the past, Yeats knows, he dealt with life in terms of legend; his work was ornate, dreamy, fanciful. But too many imitators debased his style, and so he sees, now, that "there's more enterprise in walking naked"—in stripping away decoration and letting the fierce bones of reality show through. Of course Yeats was, more than any other poet of the century, to make up *new* myths for himself, to wear metaphysical masks and hide behind mystical dominos. But at least he never again so wholly concealed the force of his passion behind curtains of silky imagery. The masks he donned from now on were as rough and bony as truth itself.

THE WILD SWANS AT COOLE

INTRODUCTION: This wonderfully various and rich volume of 1919 leads directly into the three great volumes Yeats published in the 1920's, his supreme achievement. But *The Wild Swans at Coole* contains a number of poems that are important enough in their own right. The poet emerged from the political activism and terse, stylized dryness of *The Green Helmet* and *Responsibilities* with a new profound and speculative imagination, an imagination which needed only a few new symbols and a few new experiences to begin creating great art of the major, myth-making sort. These new experiences included *the* new experience, perhaps the most significant of the poet's life—his sudden marriage in 1917 to Georgie Hyde-Lees, an attractive young woman who shared many of his esoteric interests and who responded to him with a "glad kindness" that he had never found in Maud Gonne. Though remembering that first and lifelong love the poet was dejected for a while after his marriage, he soon seems, without even being aware of it himself, to have been freed to write more vivid and various poems. Energies and intensities which had so long been channeled mainly in the one narrow direction of Maud Gonne seemed now to burst furiously forth. The political poems of *The Green Helmet* and *Responsibilities* had been a tentative start of one kind, "The Magi" and "The Cold Heaven" a start of another. Now the poet pursued these explorations more vigorously than ever before. Marriage had given him new metaphors.

Most obviously, of course, marriage liberated Yeats' sexuality, enabling him to write of sex more freely and to use it more frankly for metaphor and symbol. But the most important metaphors marriage gave the poet were (cf. General Introduction) those of *A Vision*, the elaborate occult work which was engendered when, shortly after their marriage, Georgie Yeats, to divert her husband from his deep depression, began to experiment with automatic writing. Out of these writings of his wife's—or of the poet's ghostly "instructors" who spoke through her—and out of her sleep-talking and sleep-walking, in which the instructors also played a part, came this elaborate climax to Yeats' career as an occult researcher, a book which blends semi-astrological theories of character analysis with cyclical theories of history and an intricate, rather Oriental theory of the after-life into a strange brew indeed, perhaps the most stylishly written volume of esoteric lore ever produced. But this is to get ahead of ourselves. *A Vision* was not published in its first form until 1925, and it does not therefore become really important to an understanding of the poetry until those three major volumes of the twenties which were written more or less together with it. A few of the poems at the end of *The Wild Swans at Coole* partake of *A Vision's* imagery, however (indeed, three are simply versifications of theories that were to appear in the book), and they should help us to bear in mind that by 1919 the ghostly voices had already come—as the poet later declared they did—to bring Yeats "metaphors for poetry."

"THE WILD SWANS AT COOLE": This first poem of the volume is one of the poet's best, a clear and direct lyric with a beautiful simplicity that only Yeats, in the twentieth century, has been able to manage so well. Like so much of the author's work, it deals with the problem of aging, what Unterecker has called "the anguish of mortality." Its autumnal woodland setting is reminiscent of the woodland scene and the path around the lake of "Ephemera"—but how far the poet has come since then! Then he was a pretentious boy, writing self-consciously of a weariness he could not very well have ever felt himself. Now he is a middle-aged man, genuinely "sore"-hearted, genuinely capable of reflecting, maturely, seriously and without melodrama, on the passage of time.

In the first stanza he sets the scene, describing the "autumn beauty" of trees and paths at Coole, Lady Gregory's estate, in the October twilight. It is astonishing with how few words and how bare Yeats manages vividly to evoke a complete landscape.

> Under the October twilight the water
> Mirrors a still sky;
> Upon the brimming water among the stones
> Are nine-and-fifty swans.

In the second and third stanzas he describes himself and his own relationship to the swans. It is nineteen years (stanza 2) since he first saw and counted the fifty-nine swans of this lake, nineteen years since he first saw them mounting and wheeling above him "upon their clamorous wings" as he finished his count below. And in these nineteen years (stanza 3) "all's changed" in the poet's life; nineteen years older, perhaps nineteen years sadder, he now steps with a heavier tread than he did before.

The last two stanzas describe the swans, contrasting their apparent changelessness with the terrible flux of the poet's ebbing life. They seem "unwearied," paddling the "cold companionable streams" in passionate pairs, as though "their hearts have not grown old." Drifting "on the still water" they are "mysterious, beautiful" (a daring phrase, for only Yeats could make two such overworked adjectives come so alive) and the poet wonders whose eyes they will delight when he awakes "to find they have flown away."

> **COMMENT:** The swans swimming the still water in their changeless pattern are another example of the kind of luminous elusive image that Yeats learned from the symbolists. Graceful but fierce and passionate, they seem to represent both the perfect intensity of youth and, in the changelessness of their pattern, the perfect pattern of art, which preserves youth in "the artifice of eternity." Yet they are not so limitedly or specifically defined as to make the poem only or even primarily a meditation about art. Forever "mysterious, beautiful" the swans symbolize also the flux and the fixedness of life, for though individual swans die, the pattern of fifty-nine swans remains. Dying, the old swans are replaced by younger ones, and so the swans are both changing and changeless. A swan dies, but the swans live, and as the new are indistinguishable from the old, the swans become an intricate symbol of youth, forever passing yet forever renewed. When the poet's youth—it may be his life itself—flies away like the swans, youth itself will still remain, for there will still be young men to gaze in wonder at the still pools and fifty-nine clamorous swans to delight their eyes.

"OUR SIDNEY AND OUR PERFECT MAN":   "The Wild Swans at Coole" was set at Lady Gregory's country estate, and the next two poems—"In Memory of Major Robert Gregory" and "An Irish Airman Foresees His Death"—also deal with a subject relating to Lady Gregory, her son and Yeats' friend Major Robert Gregory, a talented painter, a skillful horseman, a scholarly, gifted young man who was killed in World War I. "In Memory of Major Robert Gregory," the first of these two poems, is a superficially casual, conversational elegy which closer study reveals to be a breathtaking technical achievement. It is rather like "The Wild Swans at Coole" in this respect, for though the style of both seems simple and spontaneous, rarely had "sweet sounds" been more laboriously "articulated together." The intricate stanza form of "Major Robert Gregory," for instance, sets a rhyme scheme of *aabbcddc* against a metrical scheme of 55545445, a stanza form Yeats based on one used (also in an elegy) by the seventeenth-century "metaphysical" Abraham Cowley. Yet complex as is its construction, the gist of the poem, which moves from informal observation almost to formal lamentation and back to informality again, is simple. The poet is meditatively addressing his new wife Georgie, and sadly remarks that he will name the dead friends who cannot visit them in their new home. Among this company he includes the scholarly Lionel Johnson, one of the "companions of the Cheshire Cheese" with whom he founded the Rhymers' Club; John Synge, the "passionate and simple" playwright whose creative genius Yeats respected almost more than any other; old George Pollexfen, his own grandfather, who was a renowned horseman "in muscular youth;" and last, most shockingly (for he has just recently heard the news of his death), Major Robert Gregory:

> I am accustomed to their lack of breath,
> But not that my dear friend's dear son,
> Our Sidney and our perfect man,
> Could share in that discourtesy of death.

All the countryside in which they've just settled (Thoor Ballylee, the poet's new home, was bought from Lady Gregory and was originally part of her Coole Park land), Yeats tells his wife, was loved by Robert Gregory, and near here he rode to hounds; he was swifter and stronger than any other horseman— "and yet his mind outran the horse's feet." He seemed destined to be a great painter, too, so that "soldier, scholar, horseman," he seemed to combine the wisdom, passion and strength of the first three friends Yeats mentioned in one person. Yet so perfect was he, so intensely alive, such an ideal pattern of manhood, "what made us dream that he could comb grey hair?"—that is, how could his friends have hoped for such perfection to last?

Finally, grief stricken, Yeats tells his wife that he can no longer pursue his memories of dead friends, for the "thought/Of that late death took all my heart for speech."

COMMENT: The courtly complexity of this poem reminds us most strongly of Donne and the other metaphysicals; it is no surprise to find that Yeats took the stanza form from Cowley. Actually, Yeats had, like most recent poets, long been an admirer of Donne, a poet who was only just, around the turn of the century, beginning to emerge from a long critical eclipse, and the sinewy, conversational yet intricately structured style of Donne proved an especially happy choice for this elegy. Beginning reflectively, in a low-keyed address to his wife, as casual as if the two had just seated themselves "beside a fire of turf in th'ancient tower," the poet—first recollecting his dead old friends of long ago and then moving from these to the more recent and therefore more painful hurt of Robert Gregory's death—gradually builds to a fierce climax of grief in stanzas 9, 10 and 11. The phrase, "Soldier, scholar, horseman, he . . . (etc.)," which is repeated, each time with a more extravagant ending in each of the three stanzas, may rather remind us of the passionate refrain which knits together Donne's elegy for Elizabeth Drury, "The First Anniversary:" "Shee, shee is dead, shee's dead; when thou knowst this/Thou knowst how ugly a monster this world is;" (or "how lame a cripple this world is," and etc., with various endings). But while Donne's lines are general, philosophic in their approach to death, never individualizing the girl who is mourned (like, indeed, most formal elegies, e.g. "Lycidas," "Adonais," etc., which deliberately efface the personality of the dead man, mythologizing him, as it were, from the first), Yeats' refrain, like his poem, is firmly founded on the unique talents of Major Gregory, the traits that most distinguished him from others. On the basis of these characteristics, which the poet carefully establishes, the dead man is finally made, in stanza 11, into a kind of legend, "as 'twere all life's epitome," a dream of mortal perfection which, like all mortal dreams, must necessarily be fleeting.

The metaphor Yeats uses in this stanza (11) to generalize the individual Robert Gregory into such a pattern of perfection is a striking one, a true metaphysical conceit.

> Some burn damp faggots, others may consume
> The entire combustible world in one small room
> As though dried straw, and if we turn about
> The bare chimney is gone black out
> Because the work had finished in that flare.
> Soldier, scholar, horseman, he,
> As 'twere all life's epitome.
> What made us dream that he could comb grey hair?

Unlike ordinary dullards, in other words, who live as long and as tamely as damp wood burns, a man of Major Gregory's brilliance does so much so well that he burns himself out early. By extension, of course, Yeats seems to be saying that the best die young—and certainly we might agree that the more skillful and talented a man is, the more he does and wants, the more risks he takes. A man of Gregory's stamp, thought Yeats, was so passionate and brilliant that he brought on himself the final risk—the risk of consuming "the entire combustible world in one small room." Thus he becomes an image of perfection that is, by paradoxical necessity, self-destroying, of youth consumed, as it were, by its own promise (was it not his courage that made him a soldier?), of mortality that is all the more surely and swiftly doomed the closer it comes to immortal perfection.

"An Irish Airman Foresees His Death," the second of these two Major Gregory poems, is a brief lyric, supposedly spoken by Gregory himself—or any courageous Irish aviator. Speculating on the cause that has brought him into his perilous position "among the clouds," knowing that he will die there ("those that I fight I do not hate,/Those that I guard I do not love"), the speaker finally decides that "a lonely impulse of delight"—the fierce gaiety of heroism, which always fascinated Yeats so much —drove him to "this tumult," and that, indeed, both the past and the future seemed futile, "a waste of breath," in comparison to "this life, this death," this brief but intense life in the sky, this meaningful because heroic death among turbulent clouds.

> **COMMENT:**   A poem about balance and balancing, this lyric brilliantly illustrates the logic of Yeats' mind. The word "balance" itself appears twice ("I balanced all, brought all to mind . . . In balance with this life, this death") reminding us that the speaker is not only making a decision which requires sure moral balance but also literally balancing high in the sky, hawklike, in the clouds high above the world of men. Furthermore, through a series of paired ideas, words and images, the theme of balance becomes an integral part of the working out of the poem, of its intellectual structure and even its syntax ("those that I fight/those that I guard . . . ," "Kiltartans Cross . . . /Kiltartan's poor," " . . . could bring them loss/ . . . or leave them happier . . . ," "Nor law nor duty . . ./Nor public men . . . ," "the years to come,/the years behind," "this life, this death," etc.) And though such a listing of the balanced pairs may make them seem mechanically contrived, they do not seem so within the context of the poem. Rather they contribute to the air both of breathless expectation and of grave decision with which Yeats imbues the speaker. The poem gives us a sense of a life hanging in the balance, of a man being weighed in the balance and being found not wanting.

AGING: A number of the poems in *The Wild Swans at Coole* that follow these three remarkable opening pieces deal with Yeats' familiar theme of aging. Now Yeats speaks with a new sincerity of his old subject. When he wrote *Oisin* he was still a young man, after all, only anticipating the ills that age could bring. Now, in his fifties, he fears that his earlier vision is about to become a reality. In the ironically titled "Men Improve with the Years," "The Living Beauty," and "A Song," he complains that he can no longer respond to a woman's beauty as he used to. "O would that we had met/When I had my burning youth!" he cries, ("Men Improve"), and then, "O who could have foretold/That the heart grows old?" (A Song"). Perhaps some of these verses were written in the difficult period just after his marriage, when he feared that he could not give his young wife the passion he had expended in a lifetime's devotion to Maud Gonne.

"Under the Round Tower" is a ballad-like poem, in the mode of the "Beggar" poems of *Responsibilities*, which fictionalizes Yeats' dream of perfect love in Billy's vision of a "golden king" and a "wild lady" who sing "like a brace of blackbirds." In the next poem, "Solomon to Sheba," we hear their song—a discourse, fittingly, of love, for they "have found/There's not a thing but love can make/The world a narrow pound." "To a Young Beauty" and "To a Young Girl" were both written for Iseult Gonne, and since they are directed to her from the vantage point of Yeats' experienced maturity, they may be said also to deal with aging —with the contrast between age and youth. "The Scholars," too, is based on such a contrast: on the ironic contrast between "old, learned, respectable bald" scholars who "edit and annotate" the poems "rhymed out in love's despair" by passionate young men.

PASTORALS: "Shepherd and Goatherd," which appears about halfway through this volume, is another elegy for Robert Gregory, this time written more or less in the form of a pastoral elegy, an elegy set in dialogue between two traditional rural characters, a shepherd and a goatherd, who mourn the death of one of their number, a brilliant young shepherd (Robert Gregory) who "had thrown the crook away/And died in the great war beyond the sea." It is especially notable for its use of the dialogue form, a technique which Yeats (perhaps as a result of his play-writing) was to use again in some of his most brilliant future poems. The goatherd's song—"He grows younger every second"—should be read with special care, for it is a perfect, versified description of what Yeats declared in *A Vision* to be the after-life process, the process by which the soul unwinds its life's memories until it returns, naked of knowledge, to the great spiritual darkness, the cosmic trance, the vast oblivion, from which it sprang.

"The Fisherman," another poem on a pastoral subject, describes

Yeats' ideal audience, the man to whom, "in scorn of this audience" of clowns and critics, he would like to address his poems—a kind of peasant aristocrat who skillfully fishes the cold mountain streams, "a man who does not exist/A man who is but a dream." But be he dream or not, the poet cries that "Before I am old/I shall have written him one/Poem maybe as cold/And passionate as the dawn."

> **COMMENT:**   Though Yeats postulates him as an audience, the fisherman seems to be a kind of symbol of the poet himself, fishing in the wild streams of his mind, "where stone is dark under froth." Thus his ideal audience is in a sense his ideal self—strong, cold, reserved, heroic—and to this audience, he would like to address his ideal poem, a poem which combines, paradoxically, purity of language and form (coldness) with intensity of vision (passion) just as dawn combines the coldness of the night just past with the radiance of the rising sun.

MAUD GONNE AND OTHERS: "Her Praise," "The People," "His Phoenix," "A Thought From Propertius," "Broken Dreams," and "Presences" are all poems either for or about Maud Gonne. The last, "Presences," also refers to two other woman: a "harlot," (an unnamed woman who seduced the poet and tried to get him to marry her by asserting that she was pregnant), and a "child" (Iseult Gonne, to whom he at one time proposed marriage). "A Queen" is, of course, Maud Gonne herself. "Upon a Dying Lady" is a brilliant set of verses written about the beautiful Mabel Beardsley, younger sister of the nineties painter and writer, Aubrey Beardsley, who was now, at the age of forty-two, dying of cancer. Yeats visited her regularly and admired the fantastic gaiety and courage with which she endured terrible sufferings. The "great enemy" of poem number VII is, of course, death itself.

MASK AND METAPHYSIC: The remaining poems in *The Wild Swans at Coole* deal with the various theories Yeats was busy developing at this time, either in separate essays or in *A Vision*. *Ego Dominus Tuus* is another dialogue poem, this time a dialogue between *Hic*, an objective, "solar" (realistic), scientific, modern speaker, and *Ille*, a subjective, "lunar" (dreamy), traditional speaker, much more like Yeats himself. While *Hic*, in the modern manner, is anxious to "find myself and not an image"— that is, to know and understand his own reality—*Ille*, who speaks for Yeats, dramatically calls "to my own opposite," in the belief that by *seeming* rather than *being*, by wearing the mask of his anti-self, he can create a truth higher than bare reality, for "art is but a vision of reality," not the thing itself. And in the end the anti-self to whom *Ille*—that is, Yeats—calls, is the "mysterious one who yet/Shall walk the wet sands by the edge of the stream/ And look most like me, being indeed my double,/And prove of all imaginable things/The most unlike . . ." The fisherman, skillful and silent in the cold dawn, is the opposite of the studious poet in his book-filled tower, and it is he who can, therefore, fortify the poet-scholar's life with all the strength of his lonely yet somehow heroic activity.

"The Phases of the Moon," not a particularly effective poem in itself, is a versified dialogue between two characters who appear in Yeats' preface to *A Vision*; here, standing beneath the window of the poet's tower at night, they set forth their theories of the relationship between the moon's waxing and waning and the soul's activity. Carefully expressed as they are, these theories are simply a form of astrological character analysis (with phases of the moon substituted for the more frequently used constellations and planetary "influences" as determinants of personality) and they can be found in a more elaborate form in Book I of *A Vision*. Yet this poem, as well as "The Cat and the Moon," and "The Saint and the Hunchback," does have a certain undeniable power above and beyond the magnetism of the language. Perhaps it is the power of the central moon imagery, which became so distinctively Yeatsian, for the moon that mysteriously controls the tides of the powerful sea is a brilliant metaphor for all the troubling, mysteriously unknowable cosmic forces that have made man what he is. Passing from phase to phase, it symbolizes the flux and fickleness of life, eternally changing, evolving, ungraspable, unstoppable, yet eternally fixed in the same natural patterns.

"Two Songs of a Fool" is another of Yeats' poems in the "Beggar" mode, a difference being that here he recognizes that even the humblest and simplest creatures—like fools or beggars—have responsibilities (looking back to the earlier volume of that name). "Another Song of a Fool" is about reincarnation, "the sweet and harsh" bell being the schoolmaster's death knell. "The Double Vision of Michael Robartes," the final poem in the section, introduces for almost the first time what was to become a central image in Yeats, the image of the dancer who, caught here between the Sphinx (Intellect) and the Buddha (Heart) dances with superhuman grace, transcending flesh—a symbol of art, perhaps, or of all the patterns of perfection men fix in "the artifice of eternity." Yeats had used dancers in his early work, of course—faeries were almost always dancing on his level shores, or on his islands or in his woods—but now the faery dance had become human, an expression of imperfect man's divine potential.

MICHAEL ROBARTES AND THE DANCER

INTRODUCTION: This rather brief volume of 1921 nevertheless contains several of Yeats' most famous poems and was written when the poet was at the height of his mature powers. Marriage, as we have seen, released much of Yeats' creative energy, providing him—through *A Vision*—with new "metaphors" for poetry and freeing him from the by now rather barren subject of his "barren passion" for Maud Gonne. Of course Yeats did continue to write some verses in which the now widowed Madame MacBride appeared, but the days of frustrated and fruitless devotion were over; the proud, fierce, enigmatic beloved was no longer at the heart of his work.

Politics continued to interest Yeats—and indeed, even if he hadn't been interested they would have forced themselves into consideration, for Ireland since the famous Easter rising of 1916 had been in the midst of her political "troubles," the violent fighting and upheaval which lasted for almost a decade and finally ended with the country's establishment as an independent nation-state in 1922. Narrowly *partisan* politics, however, did not absorb Yeats as they had in the past—as when he wrote his Lane pictures poems, for instance. Now he confined himself mainly to comment on the basic philosophical theories behind specific events, on the large historical movements out of which events grew, or, most often, on their personal implications. Everything, however—love poems, autobiographical poems, ballads, dialogues and other narrative verses, historical and political poems—was informed with the intensely speculative imagination that was simultaneously engaged in organizing *A Vision*. Yeats' interest in the occult had been lifelong; in around 1910, dissatisfied with the hermetic and esoteric movements he'd already explored, the poet had turned to spiritualism and began attending seances regularly. Out of one of these had come his first ghostly "instructor," a spirit named Leo Africanus who had been a Moorish geographer and poet in the Middle Ages and who now claimed to be the Irish writer's opposite. Yeats produced *Per Amica Silentia Lunae* about this relationship in 1917, a short book in which he expounded his doctrine of Masks, most especially of the Mask of the Opposite. Now, miraculously, in his own home, his own bedroom, he found not one but a multitude of ghostly instructors, all of whom spoke through his wife. With mounting excitement he began to record, interpret and organize their utterances. He saw in them the possibility of an esoteric system which would make sense out of what often seems to every man the nonsense of man's fate, bring coherence out of the incoherence of history, and illuminate the darkness of the afterlife. In the end, as Yeats later saw, the system proved not "miracle, bird nor golden handiwork" but a theoretical structure derived from and related to numerous other similar astrological and philosophical ventures. But in these years, as he felt his speculative imagination free itself from the bondage of earlier, more conventional ideas and soar unfettered on the wings of what seemed a special revelation to him and him alone, Yeats was able to reach his greatest richness and strength as a poet. He had newly minted symbols into which to pour his passion and was no longer imprisoned in the sick self-consciousness of unrequited love.

THREE DIALOGUES: The first three poems in the section are dialogues, each between a man and a woman and each exploring some aspect of the male-female relationship. In the first, Yeats' protagonist, Michael Robartes, admonishes the beautiful dancer who wants to "put" herself "to college" that "all beautiful women may/Live in uncomposite blessedness . . . if they will banish every thought unless" their bodies "think it too."

> **COMMENT:**   A light, rather witty poem despite the metaphysical airs of Michael Robartes himself, this little dialogue nevertheless expresses an idea that Yeats was beginning to hold with increasing vehemence, an idea that might be summarized as "Beautiful women should be seen and not heard," for theirs is the wisdom of the body, an instinctive art based on "the bestial floor"—the physical self—and therefore more truly unified than any knowledge "mere books" can grant. Out of this central idea were to come two major kinds of poems in Yeats' later life. First, poems written in condemnation of politically active beauties (Con Markiewicz, Maud Gonne, etc.) whose intellectual activities have spoiled their real talent, the physical genius of their looks (or, conversely, poems in praise of fully integrated, non-political beauties); second, poems exploring the image of the dancer, her integration of being, her art that, expressed with and through the flesh, nevertheless transcends the flesh.

"Solomon and the Witch" celebrates the perfect love of Solomon and Sheba (who are often used as symbols for Yeats and his wife, or more generally, for the sexual adjustment of happily married couples). When Sheba, during lovemaking, cries out in a strange tongue, Solomon explains to her that a mysterious supernatural "cockerel" may be crowing in the end of the world as legend declares it will when, "chance being at once with choice at last," an ideally mated couple are united in "the bride-bed." But Sheba objects that "the world stays," and when Solomon speculates that their images may have been too strong or too weak (his theories derived from some esoteric sections of *A Vision*), she wildly exclaims "O! Solomon! Let us try again!"

> **COMMENT:** Though this poem has a clear esoteric, apocalyptic meaning, it is quite possible to consider simply its internal dramatic significance without references to external theories. Considered thus, its message is quite plainly an extension of the point of "Michael Robartes and the Dancer:" not the mind's but the body's wisdom, expressed through sex, is truly earth-shaking. Bodily—sexual—love, when it is a perfect expression of the soul (that is, when it represents perfectly *integrated* emotions), can revolutionize the world—for, as Yeats noted as early as "The Magi," the "uncontrollable mystery" is found on "the bestial floor." This is a rather Lawrentian philosophy, for D. H. Lawrence, too, saw perfect sexual intercourse, intercourse between perfectly matched partners, as a profound mystical experience. But Lawrentian or not, it is an outgrowth of the strain of new realism in the once-dreamy, idealistic Yeats, who now viewed the body as the shrine and origin of much religious mystery.

"An Image From a Past Life," the third of these dialogues, was written to reassure Yeats' wife of his "fondness" at a time when she imagined that ghosts from a past life (perhaps really ghosts, like Maud Gonne, from the past of *this* life) were trying to tear him from her. "Under Saturn" similarly reassures her of his love. He is not gloomy, moody, "saturnine," because of "lost love" (Maud Gonne again) but because he is brooding on his ancestors and "childish memories."

POLITICAL: The next five poems are political ones, originating in the Irish Easter rising of 1916. Among those killed in this tragic and abortive rebellion was Maud Gonne's once "loutish"-seeming husband, Major John MacBride, and among those taken prisoner was Yeats' beautiful childhood friend, Con Markiewicz. In "Easter 1916" he celebrated these new, saintlike heroes and heroines of nationalism, men and women whose lives had been heretofore ordinary, but whose grimly fixed purpose, like a stone in the midst of the living stream ("the stone's in the midst of all") had brought to pass a "terrible beauty" ("a terrible beauty is born")—the beauty and tragic gaiety of heroic sacrifice. "Sixteen Dead Men" tells more specifically about Irish events and the particular heroism they inspired: sixteen men were killed by the English after the uprising of Easter 1916, and Yeats argues that as a kind of logical result of "Easter 1916" their deaths have changed the political situation "utterly." Appeasement, passive acceptance, conciliation are no longer possible. "The Rose Tree" uses Yeats' old symbol of the rose in a new political context. "On a Political Prisoner" is about Con Markiewicz, a woman whom Yeats had known when she was a beautiful girl in Sligo, the poet's native county, before years of political activity had made her mind "a bitter, an abstract thing." Thus the poem combines its political concern (Con Markiewicz was imprisoned for her part in the 1916 uprising) with the idea, stated earlier in "Michael Robartes and the Dancer," that women should not destroy the natural spontaneous genius of their physical beauty with unnatural mental exertions, especially exertions of a political nature.

"THE SECOND COMING":   This, probably the most famous single poem in *Michael Robartes and the Dancer*, and one of the most widely read and anthologized of all Yeats' poems, unites the poet's political and mystical concerns in an intense and visionary artistic whole. In the first stanza the poet describes the present state of the world—its political upheavals, the chaos and cynicism of modern civilization, the haphazard brutality of contemporary culture. The first image, of the falcon (hunting hawk) losing touch with its keeper as it flies out of range of his call or whistle, summarizes all this. The fixed point, the central belief or idea, around which our civilization (like a falcon) had revolved (i.e., Christianity) has lost its power; it can no longer hold society in an orderly structure like a wheel around it (a structure which Yeats depicts as a series of gyres, or outward-spiralling circles). Instead, things are flying away, falling apart; our civilization is disintegrating.

In the second stanza the poet declares that all this chaos, confusion and disintegration must surely be a sign that a revelation, a "Second Coming" of the Messiah is at hand. And even as he says this, he experiences the extraordinary vision which is the poem's climax. He sees "a vast image out of *Spiritus Mundi*" (the world-spirit, or what the psychoanalyst Carl Jung would call the racial unconscious), a sphinx-like creature, "a shape with lion-body and the head of a man," moving inexorably across the desert. Having had such a vision, Yeats has had, as he guessed he would, a revelation—"that twenty centuries of stony sleep/ Were vexed to nightmare by a rocking cradle"—that is, that the two-thousand years-sleep of pre-Christian man was roused and troubled by the *first* coming, the coming of Christ. This moves the poet to wonder now, two thousand years later, as he waits for the second coming of such an earth-shaking new spirit, "what rough beast, its hour come round at last/Slouches toward Bethlehem to be born?"

COMMENT: More than most of Yeats' post-*Vision*

poems this one depends on the theories the ghostly instructors brought the poet—their metaphors for poetry. Specifically it depends on Yeats' cyclical theory of history, his idea that history moves in vast two thousand year cycles, each cycle representing a civilization and each one ushered in by a dramatic religio-mystical revelation of some kind; a revelation symbolized by an annunciation (mystical conception) and birth, such as the annunciation of Mary and birth of Christ (which ushered in the Christian era of 0— 2000 A.D.) and, earlier, the annunciation of Leda and birth of Helen (which ushered in the classical, Graeco-Roman era of 2000—0 B.C.) Thus the Second Coming here is not really a second coming of Christ himself, but of a new figure—in this case cruel, bestial, pitiless—who will represent the *new* era as Christ symbolized the old. Yeats was sure that the twentieth century, of which he had seen the calamitous beginning—World War I on the continent, and at home the "troubles"—would make the end of the primary, objective Christian civilization, and the beginning of a new antithetical, subjective civilization. Thus a new, rough beast is going to take Christ's place in the cradle at Bethlehem, where it will "vex" man's old sleep to a new nightmare.

"A PRAYER FOR MY DAUGHTER":   Another one of Yeats' most notable poems, this one, like "The Second Coming," mentions the chaos of the modern world. But that chaos is only of secondary importance here, for in this work, perhaps more than any other, Yeats' theories about women, first tentatively introduced in "Michael Robartes and the Dancer," are finally crystallized and fully expounded. In stanza 1 he sets the scene: as a storm rages outside Thoor Ballylee the poet paces back and forth, praying for his infant daughter (Ann Butler Yeats, his first child, born 1919). In stanza 2 he extends the storm imagery from the physical world to the world of events,

> Imagining in excited reverie
> That the future years had come,
> Dancing to a frenzied drum,
> Out of the murderous innocence of the sea.

Then in stanza 3 he begins to tell us the prayer for his child that has taken shape in his mind as he listened to the wind. The essence of it is "May she be granted beauty and yet not/Beauty to make a stranger's eye distraught". Most of the subsequent stanzas are variations on this theme, such as (stanza 4), those who are too beautiful forget to be kind, making beauty an end in itself.

Like Helen and Venus (stanza 5) they usually marry beneath them. It's better (stanza 6) to be courteous and kind, earning hearts that way, for "many a poor man" (Yeats himself, perhaps), who has loved great beauties, in the end "from a glad kindness" (Mrs. Yeats) "cannot take his eyes." May she thus (stanza 7) "become a flourishing hidden tree," living quietly in merriment and courtesy, away from the stormy fame of greater beauties, "rooted in one dear perpetual place." For the poet knows (stanza 8) that "to be choked with hate/May well be of all evil chances chief," and that (stanza 9) "an intellectual hatred" (such as that which drove Maud Gonne) is the worst and most disfiguring of vices. But (stanza 9) "all hatred driven hence/The soul recovers radical innocence/And learns at last that it is self-delighting." Finally (stanza 10), having prayed that his daughter will develop into a quiet, courteous, peaceful woman, the poet prays that her life will suit such a personality—that her bridegroom will "bring her to a house/Where all's accustomed, ceremonious," for "Ceremony's a name for the rich horn,/And custom for the spreading laurel tree."

COMMENT: "The rich horn" and "the spreading laurel tree" which appear in stanza 10 are two of the three main images of the poem. The horn of plenty, which first appears in stanza 4, is the source of all good things—of the beauty and grace with which a woman may be blessed, for instance. It is referred to again in stanza 8, specifically as the source of Maud Gonne's beauty. The laurel tree first occurs, of course, in stanza 6, when Yeats hopes that his daughter will be like that tree—flourishing in hidden peace. Thus the tree is a kind of tree of life, while laurels, too, are the ancient leaves of victory—laurel crowns. The third image, the bellows, appears in stanzas 8 and 9, and is a symbol of futile "windy" anger—the sort of "intellectual hatred" which is a curse in women (who, we will recall from "Michael Robartes and the Dancer," should rely on the spontaneous genius of their bodies, their beauty, rather than putting themselves to school). The last two lines, with their image of the tree and the horn, thus brilliantly summarize Yeats' tradition-oriented aristocratic philosophy, the love of roots and custom which we saw taking shape in "On a House Shaken by the Land Agitation" and which will reach climactic expression in "Coole Park 1919" and "Coole Park and Ballylee" in the next volume. "Ceremony," Yeats says—by which he means the whole complex of civilized courtesy which lends grace to aristocratic life—is the true source of beauty, the true horn of plenty which creates in a woman the "glad kindness" that is most to be desired. And "custom," he says—

by which he means the established tradition which orders quiet lives so gracefully and peacefully—is the true tree of life; traditions, that is, are the roots and branches of a beautiful life, just as courtesy is the source of beauty.

"A Prayer for My Daughter," one of Yeats' most intricately organized meditations on an essentially "social" subject, is rather like "In Memory of Major Robert Gregory" in several ways. First, it delineates the poet's ideal woman, just as "Major Gregory" described his ideal man. Second, like "Major Gregory," it appears considerably simpler than it actually is. In fact, it uses the same carefully articulated stanza form (*aabbcddc*—55545445) as the earlier poem, following the pattern which Yeats is alone among contemporary poets in having perfected—the seemingly casual yet carefully crafted conversational poem which, beginning with a meditation on one topic, superbly expands to include all life in its speculative range.

The last two poems of *Michael Robartes and the Dancer* are brief, almost epigrammatic verses, the first ("A Meditation in Time of War") dealing with about as general a subject as possible ("I knew that One is animate/Mankind inanimate fantasy"), the second ("To Be Carved On a Stone at Thoor Ballylee"), with as particular a subject as possible ("I the poet William Yeats . . . Restored this tower for my wife Georgie."). As such, they seem a pair of complementary opposites—like halves of a single divided whole—which perfectly represent the two sides of Yeats' poetic personality—his speculative philosophical imagination, and his nakedly personal, almost confessional intensity.

THE TOWER

INTRODUCTION: *The Tower*, published in 1928, is probably Yeats' most important single volume. Certainly it contains many of his most famous, most widely read, anthologized, quoted, studied and explicated poems, major works like "Sailing to Byzantium," "Leda and the Swan," "The Tower" and "Among School Children." Indeed, as one leafs through this section in the *Collected Poems*, one is struck by the consistently high—the brilliant—level of achievement that the poet was able to maintain throughout. Yeats, of course, was as skillful and careful a craftsman as there has been in this century, but even he, especially in earlier volumes, had off moments. Yet in *The Tower* it seems as though each poem is succeeded by one as great or greater, as though Yeats had found a kind of philosopher's stone of poetry, a magic talisman which enabled him to transmute whatever dross he happened upon into the purest literary gold.

The role of magic talisman was, as we have noted before, played at least in part by the system of metaphors and symbols that was *A Vision*. "Leda and the Swan," for instance, was written deliberately to illustrate Book V of that work, as a kind of *texte d'explication* out of which the poet might gradually develop his "annunciation" theory of history. "Sailing to Byzantium," too, depends on *A Vision*, though much less centrally than either "Leda" or its later companion-piece, "Byzantium." "All Souls' Night," of course, was originally intended as an Epilogue to *A Vision*, and so it involves, though it does not enunciate, the "mummy truths" of the book. And "Two Songs From a Play" elaborates further the historical pattern on which "Leda and the Swan" is based.

But what of the poems in *The Tower*—and they are many—which are not directly related to *A Vision*? What magic talisman, what philosopher's stone makes them—"Meditations in Time of Civil War," "Nineteen Hundred and Nineteen," "The Tower," "Among School Children,"—such towering masterpieces? The answer is that, while the first group of poems, the *Vision* poems, were produced primarily by what we have called Yeats' speculative imagination, this second group seems to stem more directly from the other side of his poetic genius, his brilliant sense of autobiography, his confessional intensity. Their secret, in other words, is a kind of inspired egotism (the secret of many great romantic poems, after all),—a meditative self-absorption which enabled the poet to transmute even the simplest objects of his daily life—his house (a tower), his garden (full of roses), his paperweight (an old Samurai sword)—into symbols of the highest order. He had certainly done this before, most notably, of course, with Maud Gonne, who became variously a symbol of beauty itself, of "fallen majesty," and of misguided womanhood. But such a use of the beloved is traditional among poets, and it wasn't until marriage "knitted" him into life (as he himself declared it did) that Yeats was able to see such gold in the dross of daily experience. Thus between the new, almost prophetic intensity that *A Vision* gave to his metaphysical symbols and speculations, and the new confidence with which marriage helped him to confront ordinary reality, Yeats was able, in *The Tower*, to attain a level of poetic achievement he had never reached before.

A third strain, however, is also present, indeed ever-present, in these poems, and this is the bitterness of Ireland's political situation, which seems to have united the first two strains we identified —prophecy and personal reality—into a third source of inspiration for the poet. Irish politics provided him, in "Nineteen Hundred and Nineteen" and "Meditations in Time of Civil War," with both a living, seemingly bottomless well of bitterness and just the right ground on which to take a gloomily prophetic stand. Indeed, sometime after *The Tower* was published Yeats wrote to Olivia Shakespeare that he was amazed by the book's "bitterness." And on the surface such bitterness does seem surprising, coming as it did from a Nobel Prize winner, a Senator, a happy husband and father. Yet looking further one sees that there was cause enough. To be a leading citizen (not yet a Senator) of a country in 1922 hopelessly divided against itself, or of a nation that was being in 1919 brutally and systematically oppressed by another was surely cause for bitterness. Even more, to have discovered some of the simplest satisfactions of life for the first time at the age of fifty was cause for bitterness, as well as, more important, an opportunity to state his oldest theme—of aging, of passing time— with fantastic new force and authority.

At last knitted into life so that he could write about it more passionately and perceptively, Yeats must have brooded on the irony of his having found this new reality—life instead of dreams— so late. Happily married and the father of two young children, he was already in his sixties, an "old coat upon a stick to scare the birds," and felt called upon to relinquish this new life just as he had discovered its joys. "The abstract joy/The half-read wisdom of daemonic images" must "suffice the aging man, as once the growing boy," he wrote. No wonder he was bitter! Yet his bitterness was magic too; it gave even more of a shine to his verses, as if it were still another aspect of the wonderful stone that turned life's mud and bones to gold. His emotional state at this time seems to have involved a curious, marvellous conjunction of fulfillment and dissatisfaction—one of those accidental combinations of circumstance and preparation which so often act upon genius to produce the greatest art.

"SAILING TO BYZANTIUM":   This first poem of *The Tower*, probably Yeats' most famous single poem, superbly expresses in its careful oppositions of age and youth, art and reality, some of the keenest central dilemmas of the book—and, indeed, some of the poet's own longest-standing preoccupations. Its main concern, of course, is Yeats' oldest theme—the subject of *The Wanderings of Oisin* and of "The Wild Swans at Coole"—aging, passing time, man's mortality. Together with "The Tower" and "Among School Children," (both poems rather more autobiographical in tone) "Sailing to Byzantium," (more purely imaginative and almost mythical in its style) forms a group of meditations on age and its implications which is at the heart of *The Tower*, informing all the rest of the book. Even those poems on completely different subjects have some of the bitter intensity of the aging poet's soul.

"Sailing to Byzantium" is quite a short poem, consisting of four rather simply put together stanzas (*ababcc*, all in roughly iambic pentameter). In the first, the poet describes the natural world, where the young of all species—birds, fish, people—are busy loving, reproducing and "commending" the flesh. Though these "generations" are "dying" from the moment of their birth, they do not notice it. "Caught" in the "sensual music" of life, they "neglect/Monuments of unaging intellect"—works of art, religion or philosophy, the products of man's non-physical imagination. But what place is there among these young sensualists for an old man whose senses have already begun to fail, his flesh to falter?

In stanza 2 Yeats describes the predicament of the old man more closely. "An aged man" is no more than a scarecrow, a "tattered coat upon a stick," unless he rejects the flesh—which has in any case become inadequate—and concentrates on improving his soul, sending it to school to learn to sing. For if, in the first stanza, we learned about the "sensual music" of nature, now we will discover that there is a corresponding spiritual music which the soul can study—the music of art, of poetry, for instance, for are not poems "monuments of [the soul's] own magnificence?" "And therefore," Yeats tells us, he has "sailed the seas [figuratively, of course] and come,/To the holy city of Byzantium," a kind of capitol of art.

COMMENT: Many critics have commented on the Byzantium poems, which are among Yeats' most famous works, and a good number of them have concentrated on analyzing the special significance of "the holy city of Byzantium" to the poet. T. R. Henn, in *The Lonely Tower*, suggests that Byzantium "has a multiple symbolic value." First, "it stands for the unity of all aspects of life, for perhaps the last time in history . . . " As Yeats himself wrote, in *A Vision*, "I think if I could be given a month of Antiquity and leave to spend it where I chose, I would spend it in Byzantium a little before Justinian opened St. Sophia and closed the Academy of Plato. I think I could find in some little wine-shop some philosophical worker in mosaic who could answer all my questions, the supernatural descending nearer to him than to Plotinus even, for the pride of his delicate skill would make what was an instrument of power to princes and clerics, a murderous madness in the mob, show as a lovely flexible presence like that of a perfect human body. I think that in Byzantium, maybe never before or since in recorded history, religious, aesthetic, and practical life were one, that architect and artificers . . . spoke to the multitude and the few alike. . . ."

In addition to this unity of imagination, Byzantium, according to Henn, "because it is in the past . . . contains in itself . . . the mysteries of the dead." And R. P. Blackmur has proposed a similar view: "Byzantium is for Yeats," he says, "the heaven of the man's mind; there the mind or soul dwells in eternal or miraculous forms; there all things are possible because all things are known to the soul . . . [it] represents both a dated epoch and a recurrent state of insight." Lastly, Henn remarks that there is, for Yeats, a correspondence between Ireland and Byzantium, that Byzantium "might well symbolize a new Ireland breaking away from its masters so that it might develop its own philosophical, religious, and artistic destiny."

In stanza 3, the poem's passionate climax, Yeats addresses the spirits of Byzantium, the "sages standing in God's holy fire/As in the gold mosaic of a wall" (an obvious reference to Byzantine art work). He begs them to "come from the holy fire" and spiral down ("perne in a gyre") to where he is, "sick with desire/And fastened to a dying animal." He wants them to "consume away" his heart, blinded with its fleshly, mortal dreams, and teach him how to be immortal—teach him the secrets of the soul and of art, of the "artifice of eternity."

In stanza 4 Yeats imagines what this immortality would be like. It is, of course, far from the traditional concept of immortality— angels choiring, etc. This is the heaven of art, where the artist himself becomes the artifact. He is out of nature now, and having rejected nature's sensual music of stanza 1 once and for all, he becomes a golden bird, supernaturally wise, who sings the soul's music—the knowledge of all the ages—to the mythical "lords and ladies of Byzantium."

COMMENT: As we have already noted, Byzantium has a number of different meanings for Yeats. Most important, it represents "the artifice of eternity," a land of the imagination, situated, in its greatest glory, at phase 15 (in terms of *A Vision*), the point of the Full Moon, where "the fury and the mire of human veins" are superseded by miracle and by "a supernatural splendour, these walls with their little glimmering cubes of blue and green and gold." Its function as a symbol of Ireland, though perhaps real, is clearly less significant than its function as the climax of a certain kind of Christian society, a city devoted to the study of "monuments of unaging intellect," and of "the Holy Wisdom." Thus, in "Sailing to Byzantium" Yeats contrasts the temporal world, the world of "sensual music," with "the holy city of Byzantium," the world of the spirit. "Whatever is begotten, born, and dies" ought not, if it wishes to transcend the cycle of "those dying generations," to "neglect/Monuments of unaging intellect." Art, imagination and eternity are identical, and though it may seem that golden birds and mosaics are simply lifeless artifacts, they are, in reality, more intensely ensouled than living flesh. The "birds in the trees" of stanza 1, though they may sing more naturally and, at times, more spontaneously, are less alive, in a profound, spiritual sense, than the artificial birds of stanza 4, which are "set upon a golden bough to sing/To lords and ladies of Byzantium/of what is past, or passing, or to come." The "sages" who dwell in the world of the spirit, no longer "fastened to a dying animal," stand "in God's holy fire/ As in the gold mosaic of a wall," and are purified within that "supernatural splendour" to the point where their own greatness, the greatness of the soul, enables them to attain immortality and a kind of omniscience.

Several critics have noted that in his *Essays* Yeats writes of a "fifth element," a supernatural one beyond and above the four natural and traditional elements, and calls it "a bird born out of the fire." (cf. Friar and Brinnin, *Modern Poetry*) The soul, freed from flesh, becomes such a bird, an artificial bird singing in the ecstatic flames of Byzantium, the "heaven of man's imagination." "Even the drilled pupil of the eye," Yeats says in *A Vision*, "when the drill is in the hand of some Byzantine worker in ivory, undergoes a somnambulistic change, for its deep shadow among the faint lines of the tablet, its mechanical circle, where all else is rhythmical and flowing, give to Saint or Angel a look of some great bird staring at miracle." And in "Sailing to Byzantium" Yeats asserts that if "Soul clap its hands and sing . . ." it rises from "a tattered coat upon a stick" and becomes such a Saint or Angel of the imagination, staring thus at miracle.

"THE TOWER":   In this, another poem about aging, Yeats approaches the subject in a more openly autobiographical way. The poem is longer, looser, less tensely and intensely mythical in its conception, depending more for effect on what we have called the poet's confessional intensity than on his speculative imagination (though that too plays a part, especially in section 3). In other words, where "Sailing to Byzantium" is rooted in imagination, in myth, "The Tower" is rooted in reality or, at the very least, in legends which preserve the semblance of reality.

In Section 1 the poet bewails the aging of his body. Though his senses are keener than ever and his imagination more passionate than before, his body will not carry him where he wants to go. Worse, it is "a sort of battered kettle at the heel" of his spirit, and he is afraid that because of its degeneration he will have to "bid the Muse go pack" and lead the abstract, passionless life of a metaphysician.

In section 2, however, he "send[s] imagination forth" to prove its undiminished power—and to examine the "images and memories" which are the foundation of his life and of the tower which represents his life. A motley crew of vivid Irish types responds to his call, and he "would ask a question of them all," for to understand the nature of his tower he must understand its background and surroundings. The aristocrat, Mrs. French, with her temporal power, is arraigned, along with Mary Hynes, the peasant beauty, with her sensual power, and Raftery, the blind poet, whose power is the ultimate, spiritual power of the artist, the power of Homer, with whom, says Yeats, "the tragedy" (of civilization and its longings) "began."

Yeats, too, has had this power of the artist, he tells us—for he himself "created Hanrahan," the duped lover, and drove him mad with "a horrible splendour of desire," but now he wonders if he still has it ("it seems that I must bid the Muse go pack") or, indeed, if he still wants it. Is he akin to that "ancient bankrupt master of this house" who was "so harried" that he could not be cheered by the power of love or of art or of hate, the powers that Mary Hynes, Raftery and Mrs. French represent? Will he, Yeats, finish *his* "dog's day" as desperate as that former master, the "decrepit age" tied to his tail dragging him to further bankruptcy, spiritual as well as physical?

A life of action held sway over the tower, Yeats tells us, before the ruinous age of its bankrupt master. "Rough men-at-arms . . . climbed the narrow stair" to a height of glory—but is their era gone? Evidently they have vanished, along with, in the end, Mrs. French, Mary Hynes, indeed all but Hanrahan, Yeats' own creation, for when he questions them in stanza 11 of section 2 his answer is "in those eyes . . . impatient to be gone . . ." All have raged against old age, as he does, but they want nothing to do with his discussion of the subject now that they are in their graves and freed from such trivial concerns. As for Hanrahan, he is Yeats' own self, as well as his work of art, for the artist's own self must always be his work of art, and thus, like Yeats, he is an "old lecher with a love on every wind" who alone can answer the great personal question of regret. Only Hanrahan, in the grave, knows whether the images of another life, a life of action, return to haunt the spirit with their unfinished business.

In section 3 Yeats takes leave, as he knows he must, of the active sensual life whose nature he examined in Section 2 and whose passing he mourned in section 1. But if he can no longer climb "Ben Bulben's back" as he once did, "with rod and fly," he can will his independent passion, the proud tradition of his tower, to younger fisherman, and more, he can will them his faith—faith in the transcendent power of spirit that has enabled him, finally, to eschew physical pleasures without regret—so that when they, too, have reached the point where action must give way to meditation they will have the faith which enables them to make what seems to be a sacrifice. The image of the nesting bird crystallizes Yeats' emotion here: throughout his earlier life of action he accumulated "layer upon layer" of "memories and images." And now, "on their hollow top," at the pinnacle of his soul's tower, he can turn from the active material world to a contemplative, wholly spiritual world. "Now shall I make my soul," he says, and now indeed, having finally rejected "the wreck of body," he is freed for the ultimate creative act, the act of artistry which surpasses the creation of Helen or of Hanrahan, the building of a spirit into what he called in "Sailing to Byzantium" the "artifice of eternity."

PERSONAL POLITICS: The next two poems, actually groups of poems, were immediately inspired by the Irish "troubles" of 1922 (the Civil War) and 1919 (the British atrocities). But at bottom they are both profoundly personal works, too, poems which simply use the political occasion as a framework in which to present ideas and emotions that had long been germinating in the poet's mind. The first of these two groups, "Meditations in Time of Civil War," is a set of seven poems or "meditations," dealing with a variety of subjects that Yeats associated with his personal and political position in these years. In the first, "Ancestral Houses," after describing the glories of aristocracy—of the traditionally elegant and sumptuous upper-class life he had so often praised (cf. "On a House Shaken by the Land Agitation," for instance)—he for the first time questions the efficacy of such a system in producing *new* nobility, wondering "What if the glory of escutcheoned doors/And buildings that a haughtier age designed . . . But take our greatness with our bitterness?" In other words, what if years of aristocratic ease simply dissipate the original crude and bitter strength of the men who founded the noble line?

In the next two poems Yeats describes his own situation, implicitly opposing the rude strength of his own house and his rough writing table to the elegant terraces of the rich. "My House" is a particularly fascinating example of his ability to make everything he touched seem significant; not only the famous tower and winding stair of his ancient farmstead, but even the old bridge, old elms and frankly symbolic roses of his garden are drenched in the poet's magic, made into "befitting emblems of adversity," of the monastic simplicity of a life dedicated to art. And in "My Table" he depicts another such emblem—the five-hundred-year-old samurai sword presented to him by a Japanese visitor, which represents the changelessness of art. "In Sato's house/Curved like new moon, moon-luminous,/It lay five hundred years." Yet unlike the moon, the sword never changed, never abandoned the fixed perfection of its shape, its beauty preserved in "the artifice of eternity." Finally, in "My Descendants" the poet asserts that whatever his children or their children do to debase their name or house, these stones of his tower—his emblems—will "remain their monument and mine."

But in "The Road at My Door," the horror and harshness of political reality begins to intrude itself upon the poet's dream of art. Some soldiers call on him and he, "caught/In the cold snows of a dream," envies them their vitality and activity, their heroic gaiety—for they are "cracking jokes of Civil War/As though to die by gunshot were/The finest play under the sun." In "The Stares Nest by My Window," and "I See Phantoms of Hatred and of the Heart's Fullness and of the Coming Emptiness," however, the poet's envy becomes pure horror. The "Stare's Nest" comments on the chaos and brutality of the times in which the artist and his family are trapped: "We are closed in, and the key is turned/On our uncertainty; Somewhere/A man is killed, or a house burned,/Yet no clear fact to be discerned." The last poem of the series, "I See Phantoms," is wholly in the prophetic vein, drawing on moon-imagery from *A Vision* and ominous historical images ("Vengeance for Jacques Molay" was a cry of the blood-bathed French Revolution) to express the terror of what Yeats believes are the times to come. At last, as he turns to climb the stair, the poet wonders if he might after all have "proved his worth" in the world of men, of political activity, rather than alone in the lonely realm of art. But the brutality (in every sense) of such a life would only have made him "pine the more," he finally concludes. Only "the abstract joy" of art, of prophecy, of occult research, the joy of the speculative imagination, can truly satisfy "the aging man, as once the growing boy."

In "Nineteen-Hundred and Nineteen," an intricate six-part poem in the same political-prophetic vein as "I See Phantoms," Yeats again tries to come to terms with the chaos and brutality of his age, an age in which "days are dragon-ridden," and "the night-mare/Rides upon sleep." The political optimism of nineteenth-century imperial Europe, indeed of all civilization, has led to nothing but this horror, the poet bitterly notes: "The night can still sweat with terror" as it did "before/We pieced our thoughts into philosophy/And planned to bring the world under a rule,/ Who are but weasels fighting in a hole." But Yeats is not content simply to describe the nightmare of modern times. As he did in "The Second Coming," he views this chaos as (literally) ominous, a sign that "the Platonic Year/Whirls out new right and wrong,/ Whirls in the old instead."—that is, that a new historical cycle is beginning. As always, such a change is accompanied by a complete loss of values ("Come let us mock at the good," the poet ironically—despairingly—declares) and by a terrible burst of violence and depravity. The wind whirling along dusty roads bears with it the depraved daughters of Herodias (cf. Yeats' note to "The Hosting of the Sidhe," quoted earlier in the section on *The Wind Among the Reeds*) and the "insolent fiend Robert Artisson," a legendary demonic spirit who "lurches past, his great eyes without thought," as a kind of living emblem of the new age, much as that "rough beast" of "The Second Coming" slouched toward Bethlehem to be born.

EPIGRAMMATIC AND HISTORICAL VERSES: *The Tower* contains a number of epigrammatic verses which are reminiscent of some of the terse, succinct utterances of *Responsibilities*. These include "The Wheel," "Youth and Age," and especially "Fragments," which is almost gnomic in quality. The style of "Two Songs From a Play" also has an epigrammatic quality, especially the second stanza of the second song. Still, these two songs, like "Leda and the Swan," are most important as central expressions of Yeats' complex, cyclical theory of history. Very briefly, in Book V of *A Vision* Yeats had expounded the notion that history moves in great two-thousand-year cycles ("Platonic Years"). Each two-thousand-year period is dominated by a single civilization, and each civilization is dominated by a specific kind of attitude, either "primary" or "antithetical," to use the exact terms of "the system." Earlier in *A Vision* Yeats defines "antithetical" man as "subjective, introverted, aristocratic, physical, concrete, imagistic," and "primary" man as "objective, extroverted, socialistic, spiritual, abstract, contemplative."

Usually, too, each two-thousand-year cycle is dominated by a myth, which expresses in semi-fictional terms the central mood of the period. Thus for the last two thousand years European society has been ordered and controlled by the Christian myth (which is now, as we saw in "The Second Coming," on the verge of total disintegration). Often, finally, the supernatural event which generates a new socio-cultural myth—and which therefore indirectly generates a whole new civilization—is a kind of annunciation, an intervention by the divine in human affairs, usually made through some kind of sexual relationship (Zeus and Leda, Mary and the Holy Ghost) between the immortal and the mortal. Yeats himself wrote in *A Vision* that "I imagine the annunciation that founded Greece as made to Leda . . . but all things are from antithesis, and when in my ignorance I try to imagine what older civilization that annunciation rejected, I can but see bird and woman blotting out some corner of the Babylonian mathematical starlight."

> **COMMENT:**   Though Yeats, as we have seen, used "Leda and the Swan" as a kind of verse preface to Book V of *A Vision*, we really do not need too elaborate an explanation of "the system" in order to see what is going on in the poem. We do not need to be told, for instance, that some huge and violent machinery of fate is operating here; "the staggering girl" who is "so mastered by the brute blood of the air" is Helen's mother, the mother of Greece and turbulence, of "the broken wall, the burning roof and tower/ And Agamemnon dead." Still, she is helpless; though she is to bear a new civilization, alone, on earth, she cannot "put on" knowledge with this power. Even Zeus, though powerful and, presumably, able to foresee this grand chain of events is, in a sense, helpless before the vast rushing movements of an historical cycle. In a sense he is as much the instrument of this cycle as Leda is. He is "indifferent" to her, and the mechanism of time and of history is indifferent to him, though it is the power that impels him upward in "a white rush" of "feathered glory" just as surely as he is the power that deals to Leda—and to Babylonian starlight—"a sudden blow." The transcendent violence of fate is present here, as it is, in Yeats' view, at all annunciations, and each great movement forward in history is stained with the "brute blood" of terror.

Mary's annunciation, in "Two Songs from a Play," is depicted in much the same terminology as Leda's, although the "Two Songs" are basically more complex poems than "Leda and the Swan." Just as "Leda and the Swan" deals with the moment of transition from Babylonian to classical civilization, however, the

"Two Songs,"—which serve as prologue and epilogue to Yeats' play, "The Resurrection"—deal with the moment of transition from classical to Christian civilization. And though we ought, perhaps, to be rather more familiar with Yeats' system to understand them than to understand "Leda," a thorough knowledge of it is still not absolutely necessary. In these poems, as Cleanth Brooks and Robert Penn Warren (in their excellent explication in *Understanding Poetry*) point out, Yeats "though emphasizing the contrast between the two civilizations . . . establishes, paradoxically, the continuity between them. The Virgin tears the heart from the slain Dionysus . . . [who represents the Graeco-Roman myth, just as Christ represents the Judeo-Christian myth.] With her child (the 'Star,' which we may take as expressing the same principle as Dionysus) she then utters her challenge to the older civilization." Dionysus was, of course, like Adonis, Orpheus, Attis and Christ Himself, a kind of dying and rising god. The heart of Dionysus, then, still beats in the body of Mary's child, and "another Troy must rise and set/Another lineage feed the crow,/Another Argo's painted prow/Drive to a flashier bauble yet . . ."

> **COMMENT:**   In "Leda and the Swan" Yeats simply depicted the workings of the historical process in a relatively straight-forward manner; in "Two Songs from a Play," however, he adds philosophy to description. Though "Magnus Annus," the Great Year of history, brings with it a tremendous and terrifying shift from "antithetical" to "primary" civilization, though the "antithetical" Roman Empire "stood appalled" while that "fierce virgin and her Star . . . called" out of "the fabulous darkness" of a rising "primary" civilization, a basic continuity and similarity between one great period and another remains. As in "Leda," the historical shift is accompanied by blood—and, indeed, there is a change of attitudes too: the "primary" man, less orderly than the "antithetical" man, brings "a fabulous formless darkness in" and makes "all Platonic tolerance vain/And vain all Doric discipline." "Pity and not love," as Friar and Brinnin suggest, "is now the ruling force of the new civilization as the coming of Christ in agony and blood destroys the harmony, discipline and tolerance by which the Greeks lived." Still, however, man remains profoundly himself, though constantly enriched and revitalized by these changes. As Brooks and Warren remark, "Instead of the static idea of the vanity of all human glory—the fall of the mighty, the feebleness of man's might—the poem expresses a dynamic idea, an idea of development and fulfillment in this process."

"AMONG SCHOOL CHILDREN":   Starting out, like "The Tower" and "Sailing to Byzantium," as a poem about the problems of aging, "Among School Children," another one of Yeats' most famous and difficult works, ends up as a great statement—maybe the poet's greatest—on the ultimate nature of reality. As he walks through the schoolroom, perhaps comparing the fresh young faces of the children he sees to his own, aged, "scarecrow" figure, the poet—now "a sixty-year-old smiling public man" (stanza 1), an Irish senator—cannot help remembering that he, too, was young once, and that his Ledean, one-time beloved, Maud Gonne (as beautiful as the legendary Leda), was also once a beautiful "living child" (stanzas 2 and 3). Yet now (stanza 4) she is as old and "hollow of cheek" as he himself. Thus the problem of life's seeming discontinuity—the central issue of the poem—poses itself to him in stanza 5. What young mother, betrayed by the sweetness of "generation" (by which Yeats means, as Blake did, the whole reproductive *process* of life) into the pain of childbirth, would think her pain worthwhile if she could see her son as he must inevitably become, an aged scarecrow of sixty or so? In stanzas 6 and 7 the poet contemplates some of the solutions men have proposed to this puzzling—and heartbreaking—problem of life's discontinuity. Plato, for instance, thought nature didn't matter anyway, since it was only a pale shadow of the ideal. And nuns, like those who keep this schoolroom, worship saintly images of changelessness—which, however (perhaps because of their very perfection) break hearts just as surely as the doomed mortal children on whom mothers spend all their passion.

At last, in stanza 8, the poet proposes his own solution, a solution which reminds us of the central image of "The Wild Swans at Coole." One must accept reality for what it is, at once changing and changeless but always unified. The whole is more than the sum of its parts, just as the pattern of fifty-nine swans, though it depended for its existence on fifty-nine particular swans, transcended the individual members of the flock. The "great-rooted" chestnut tree is neither the leaf, the blossom, nor the bole, but all three put together in a larger whole, a single, organically—rather than mechanically—interrelated unit of life. So, too, the dancer cannot be separated from her dance, for neither could exist without the other. It is the dancer, after all, who gives body to the dance, and the dance which brightens the glance of the dancer.

COMMENT: We have encountered this central image of the dancer before, most notably in "The Double Vision of Michael Robartes" and "Michael Robartes and the Dancer," and we will again, in some important later poems. As we have already noted, she seems to represent Yeats' increasing absorption in the reality of the flesh. Thus, even here in *The Tower*, this anguished section of the *Collected Poems*, in which he seems to have completely rejected the aging, inadequate flesh and all it stands for, Yeats cannot entirely forget that art—the pattern of eternity through which he believes man can escape his body's mortal imperfections—is and must inevitably be rooted in physical reality. Of this inescapable relationship between art and the flesh the dancer, whose art *is* the flesh, is, of course, a perfect symbol. And furthermore, because of her unique relationship to her art —the necessary unity which makes the dancer and the dance inevitably one—she becomes, too, a perfect symbol of the ultimate unity of all life, of the important truth that beneath the seeming discontinuity of child and old man there is always a single whole, the one individual remaining profoundly and consistently himself through all of his life's various ages and stages.

PERSONAL REMINISCENCES: "Owen Aherne and His Dancers," though the characters are disguised, is a poem about Yeats' love life, a kind of verse the poet had not written too much of lately. He actually composed it, he later revealed, shortly after his marriage to Georgie, when he regretted not having more vehemently urged Iseult Gonne to marry him. And "A Man Young and Old" is a series of simple poems about the joys and sorrows of youth and age which draw, of course, quite considerably on the poet's long experience with Maud Gonne. In its stripped narrative style, brief simple ballad-like verses, nakedly personal intensity, moving and passionate use of madness and old age, it points the way toward Yeats' future style and toward many of his future triumphs, specifically its later companion-piece, "A Woman Young and Old," and the Crazy Jane series.

"MUMMY TRUTHS": Though "Owen Aherne" and "A Man Young and Old" have been digressions into physical reality, albeit bitter ones, the concluding note of *The Tower*, like the opening one (i.e. "Sailing to Byzantium") is determinedly spiritual. In "All Souls' Night," a magnificent, intricately versified invocation of the poet's dead friends—reminiscent of "The Grey Rock" or, even more, of "In Memory of Major Robert Gregory"—Yeats expresses his excitement at the "mummy truths," the secret esoteric knowledge ("mummy" both because long-buried and because heretofore concealed beneath the many-layered surface of reality), that he has discovered in *A Vision*. Thus the dead friends he calls on are all his friends of the occult movement, men and women who would be interested to know that "wound in mind's wandering/As mummies in the mummycloth are wound," Yeats feels that he has at last discovered some kind of ultimate truth. (The poet revealed this "truth" in *A Vision* rather than the poem). Free at last (so he thinks) of the flesh's importunate demands, he asserts of his truth: "that in it bound/I need no other thing." He later declared that the ghostly instructors of *A Vision* had come to bring him "metaphors for poetry," so might they not in a sense then be the true "singing masters" of his soul, the sages on whom he called in the first poem of this book, "Sailing to Byzantium?" If so, then his prayer was answered and now, in the holy land, he was singing—or so he believed—the holiest truths of time.

THE WINDING STAIR

INTRODUCTION: Yeats began to put this 1933 volume together in 1927, when *The Tower* itself was still only in galleys. It serves, as John Unterecker has noted, as a kind of answer to that earlier volume. Sick and weak, Yeats "suddenly realized that he might die," writes Unterecker. "But he felt, the pattern of life and work was not complete. *The Tower* had been a distortion, half the picture, its emphasis on a man making his soul; flesh, too, demanded its due. Life, the silken sheath, a woman young and old, the immortality of generation, body surviving through body—all these needed to be sung. And Yeats fought to gain strength to sing them."

Of course, as we already observed (in connection with "Among School Children"), even in his bitterest moments of revulsion against the flesh in *The Tower*, Yeats still could not forget that the dance depends upon the body of the dancer. And even in "Sailing to Byzantium," when he determinedly sails away from the land of generation, the world of the flesh, to the heaven of the imagination, he only does so because "that is no country for old men." Yet for the young, he knows, the "sensual music" of the flesh can hardly be rivalled by any spiritual music, no matter how sweet. Finally, we must conclude, Yeats saw that the flesh and the spirit must be carefully balanced against each other, held in a sane equilibrium. For art depends on physical reality as surely as the spirit depends upon the flesh for the experiences and perceptions which are the raw material of thought. Thus to reject generation—the whole cycle of physical experience—would be to reject the ultimate source of all good, of the spirit's as well as the body's song. Life's blessing is the strange, almost indefinable relationship between such seeming opposites as soul and substance, sword and sheath, dance and dancer.

OF TIME AND TIMELESSNESS: Though the three important

poems which open *The Winding Stair* seem superficially quite unlike in style and theme, all three are linked together by a common concern with the meaning of time and timelessness. The first, for instance, "In Memory of Eva Gore-Booth and Con Markiewicz," two beautiful friends of Yeats' youth, elegizes not the sisters themselves (who were actually still alive) but the innocent and lovely girls they once were. Now, like the poet himself, ruined by the natural ravages of time, and also ruined by the unnatural vehemence of futile political activity, the two "dear shadows" of their one-time selves know at last "all the folly of a fight/With a common wrong or right," and that "the innocent and the beautiful/Have no enemy but time."

> **COMMENT:**   Yeats feels, as he declared also in "Michael Robartes and the Dancer" and in "A Prayer for My Daughter," that a beautiful woman is in and of herself a work of genius, of natural art, as it were, and that for her to attempt any activities other than those which spontaneously flower from her beauty, is to be utterly self-destructive. Politics, for instance, with its pointless feuds and essentially futile quarrels, plots, revolutions and counter-revolutions, is a complete waste of loveliness and talent. Time, not any party, class or individual, is the great enemy, and if there is to be any revolution, the poet ironically concludes, it should be a revolution against "the great gazebo" of time, not the lovely "gazebo" of aristocratic tradition against which "they"—the enraged masses—have directed all their fury.

In "Death," however, Yeats declares his certainty that time can, in fact, be transcended. Only men fear death, the poet asserts; animals instinctively know that it is not to be feared, that the soul is part of an eternal cycle of incarnations which ends in final immortality. Thus in a sense it may be said that man himself has "created death," for at least he has created the false idea of a fearful and perhaps final extinction which he awaits with such a terrible mixture of dread and hope.

Finally, in "A Dialogue of Self and Soul"—really the great central philosophical utterance of *The Winding Stair*—Yeats confronts the opposed alternatives of time and timelessness and, in a triumphant affirmation of the blessed reality of life, he chooses a real existence *in time* in preference to the "breathless" timelessness of the soul. Thus section 1 of the poem is a true dialogue between the poet's Self—that is, his real but transient bodily incarnation as William Butler Yeats—and his Soul, the eternal, nameless spirit which has informed all his incarnations. But the second section is no longer a dialogue; it is the Self's hymn of praise to life, one of the poet's greatest statements of reconciliation to the often painful and frustrating but always blessed physical world which had so embittered him in *The Tower*.

In stanza 1 of section 1, the Soul describes "the winding ancient stair" which gives this volume its title and is here used as an emblem for the soul's ascent out of material existence into the final darkness, the cosmic trance (cf. the Goatherd's Song in "Shepherd and Goatherd") in which it will at least be freed from the burden of life's "memories and images." But in stanza 2 the Self reminds the Soul that Sato's changeless ancient blade (cf. "Meditations in Time of Civil War," poem 3, "My Table,") is still encased in a tattered piece of silk, a fragment of an old court-lady's dress which can, though "tattered, still protect, faded, adorn." Like this scrap of silk, the body, and the body's life, no matter how aged and battered, can still protect and adorn the eternal and changeless sword of the soul.

Scornfully the Soul replies, in stanza 3, that a man "long past his prime" should not think of life—of love and war—but "of ancestral night," which can deliver "from the crime of death and birth." But the Self still dwells on that great "crime"—life, the day—which it opposes to "the tower/Emblematical of the night," and finally demands "as by a soldier's right/A charter to commit the crime once more" (that is, to live again). The Soul, however, continues to brood on ancestral night, insubstantial Heaven, the idea of which, though, very significantly strikes it dumb. "When I think of that my tongue's a stone," the Soul is forced to confess.

But if the Soul is struck dumb by the thought of transcending life, the Self is moved to magnificent song by the thought of life itself. All of section 2 consists of this great hymn of praise. The poet is prepared to endure all the pains of life again—the "toil of growing up," the "ignominy of boyhood," the "mirror of malicious eyes," the "folly of love," etc.—and prepared, too, to "measure the lot, forgive myself the lot!" For

> When such as I cast out remorse
> So great a sweetness flows into the breast
> We must laugh and we must sing,
> We are blest by everything,
> Everything we look upon is blest.

COMMENT: One cannot help noticing how strikingly this blissful new reconciliation-to-life of Yeats' contrasts with the guilt and misery he expressed so many years earlier in a poem like "The Cold Heaven" (cf. *Responsibilities*), in which he "took the blame out of all sense or reason" for his failure with Maud Gonne. Now he can forgive himself the lot, casting out all the remorse for those unhappy years of his youth when he threw his soul at the feet of a woman who could not or would not accept the offering. More than a decade of happy marriage and fulfillment of every kind —literary, philosophical, personal—has intervened, and the poet is ready at last, old and sick as he is, to accept life with all its painful possibilities, and, more, to praise and to bless everything he looks upon. His final choice, in *The Winding Stair*, is of reality rather than art or dreams (though, significantly, it is real life which enables the Self to sing, while the Soul is struck dumb by eternity), of the Self rather than the Soul, of the flesh rather than the spirit, of time rather than timelessness. And though he will always vacillate between the two sets of alternatives, he will never again so vehemently reject his body—as he did in *The Tower*—as no more than "a battered kettle at the heel" of his spirit.

HISTORY, THE SYMBOLISM OF TIME: In the next twelve poems the poet continues to deal with aspects of time and time-lessness, only now he focuses more specifically on man's history and his own, treating it almost as a kind of symbol-system, a set of emblems of man's progress in time. "Blood and the Moon," for instance, deals with the representative history of Yeats' own race, and with the balance of thought and power in Ireland. Great Irish thinkers like Goldsmith and Swift, Berkeley and Burke, Yeats asserts, have traveled up the winding ancestral stair of his tower, making it a symbol of the ultimate wisdom toward which the Irish people ought to strive. Blood, on the other hand, represents temporal power, the "bloody, arrogant power" that so often seems to inspire and "master the race." Thus, in section 4, such blood and such power, are seen as the property of the living, while wisdom, like the moon's glory, belongs to the illustrious dead.

The next three poems—"Oil and Blood," "Veronica's Napkin" and "Symbols"—elaborate these almost occult symbols of power and wisdom, body and soul further. Then, in "Spilt Milk," "The Nineteenth Century and After," and "Three Movements," the poet turns from such metaphors to a more specifically literary view of history. The "great song" of our civilization is over and, as Matthew Arnold noted in "Dover Beach," the wave of Christianity is receding. Yet, Yeats remarks—rather ironically, we must admit—there's still "keen delight in what we have:/the rattle of pebbles" on the empty shore of time where, modern fish —like the meaningless disconnected images of modern art and thought—"lie gasping" in despair. Finally, in "The Crazed Moon," Yeats represents this general historical movement in the astrological terms of *A Vision*. The moon, which has exhausted itself with its fecund evolution of so many historical phases (and literally with itself evolving through so many phases) "staggers" through the sky like a woman made mad and weak and sick by too much childbearing. And, like the moon, our civilization seems to Yeats to have exhausted all its possibilities and to be utterly worn out.

This group of symbolic-historical poems is rounded out by a last pair of lyrics in honor of Yeats' beloved one-time patroness, Lady Gregory. In both of these—both "Coole Park, 1929" and "Coole Park and Ballylee, 1931"—the poet celebrates the sanctuary Augusta Gregory provided, amid the chaos of modern times, for artists of all sorts. Indeed, though in "Ancestral Houses" Yeats seemed to have rejected his old ideal of aristocracy, he here revives it, praising the house of which Lady Gregory is "a last inheritor/Where none has reigned that lacked a name and fame/ Or out of folly into folly came." In fact, he declares, he and she and their friends were "the last romantics—chose for theme/ Traditional sanctity and loveliness;

> Whatever's written in what poets name
> The book of the people; whatever most can bless
> The mind of man or elevate a rhyme;
> But all is changed, that high horse riderless,
> Though mounted in that saddle Homer rode
> Where the swan drifts upon a darkening flood.

COMMENT: "That high horse" is, of course, Pegasus, the holy colt of the earlier "Fascination of What's Difficult." And the evocative last couplet of the poem refers to Homer's penetration—through poetry—of the soul's deepest mysteries, the mysteries of life and death ("the darkening flood"), for the swan is generally a symbol of the soul (cf. stanza 3 of this same poem). The lines are, of course, enriched by the memories of Zeus and Leda that the Homer-swan association also calls up.

DEATH: In "At Algeciras—A Meditation Upon Death," "Mohini Chatterjee" and "Byzantium" Yeats abandons the specifics of man's history again for a renewed concentration on death as a metaphysical phenomenon. "Byzantium" is, of course, the most interesting of these poems, echoing as it does the earlier "Sailing to Byzantium." In fact, of all the poems in *The Winding Stair*—most of which celebrate time rather than timelessness— "Byzantium" is probably the only important one to reiterate *The Tower's* praise of "the artifice of eternity." For, indeed, though it seems to be a poem about death and the "dreaming back" process of the after life (cf. "Shepherd and Goatherd," and "All Soul's Night"), it is more truly, like its earlier companion, a poem about art. Thus it is concerned, like the earlier poem, with a view of the city of Byzantium as symbolic of eternity and the imagination, but, unlike "Sailing to Byzantium," it draws much of its imagery from *A Vision* and is therefore far more complex and difficult.

> **COMMENT:**   A kind of transition from one poem to the other is provided by an earlier version of "Sailing to Byzantium" in which some of the basic ideas of "Byzantium" appear:

> But now these pleasant dark-skinned mariners
> Carry me toward that great Byzantium
> Where all is ancient, singing at the oars
> That I may look in the great church's dome
> On gold-embedded saints and emperors
> After the mirroring waters and the foam
> Where the dark drowsy fins a moment rise
> Of fish that carry the souls to paradise.

And in his Diary for April 30, 1930, Yeats wrote: "Subject for a poem . . . Describe Byzantium as it is in the system towards the end of the first Christian millenium. A walking mummy. Flames at the street corners where the soil is purified, birds of hammered gold singing in the golden trees, in the harbour, offering their backs to the wailing dead that they may carry them to paradise." The "fish that carry the souls to paradise" in the earlier version of "Sailing to Byzantium" are, in "Byzantium," pictured as dolphins; the golden birds "offering their backs to the wailing dead" in Yeats' diary, become, in "Byzantium" these same dolphins. Byzantium is viewed in "Sailing to Byzantium" as a city entirely eternal and heavenly; in "Byzantium" it is seen in a state of flux, inhabited by both the living and the dead.

The poem opens when night has fallen upon the city. "The great cathedral gong," a symbol of both religion and a kind of mortal sensuality, tolls out the hours. We are at either phase 1 or phase 15 of the moon: dark of the moon, or full moon. Humanity cannot exist at either phase, and the spirits of the dead, involved in a process of purification, begin to drift in from the sea, carried by dolphins from paradise to earth and back again. "The fury and the mire of human veins" is now engulfed by "the super-human . . . death-in-life and life-in-death." "Hades bobbin bound in mummy-cloth" is each soul, spinning away, as it were, "the mortal coil," and rising to a kind of miracle. A reciprocal relationship is set up between the realm of the unpurged living and the realm of the dead. If the spirits of the dead must recede before the crowing of "a terrestrial cock," then the stained spirits of the living must now recede before the crowing of "the cocks of Hades," and before the crying of golden artificial birds, which are, in Byzantium, the earthly counterparts of the miraculous dead.

"At midnight on the Emperor's pavement," the "condition of fire," a state of purification, is dominant. ". . . blood-begotten spirits come/And all complexities of fury leave,/Dying into a dance,/An agony of trance,/An agony of flame that cannot singe a sleeve. The spiritual fire of "life-in-death" flickers throughout the city as "spirit after spirit" arrives from the sea and burns upon the "marbles of the dancing floor."

But the poem does not conclude with a state of rest, of ultimate holiness. "Those images" (used here in two senses—the almost Platonic "images" or forms of the dead, and the inspired images of the poet's vision) "beget" fresh images and the process flames on by the shores of "that dolphin-torn, that gong-tormented sea." The sea of change which separates life and death is torn by the dolphins because they are, as it were, the ferries which bear spirits from Byzantium to paradise. The sea is tormented by gongs because "all life goes to the barbarous clamor of a gong," as Yeats wrote earlier in "Nineteen Hundred and Nineteen" (and also, according to some critics, because religious ritual alone tolls in the dead, tolls out the living, and because sensuality will continue to torture those in the state between absolute flesh and ultimate spiritual purity). The only earthly process that can "break the flood"—that is, arrest it and capture its essence—is the process of art, of imagination, which is represented by "the golden smithies of the Emperor." Just as, in "Sailing to Byzantium," God's "holy fire" smoldered in "the gold mosaic of a wall," in "Byzantium" only "miracle, bird, or golden handiwork" is as free as the dead are from "all complexities of mire or blood."

LIFE IN TIME: Almost all the rest of the poems in *The Winding Stair* deal with and celebrate the body's blessed, imperfect life, the life in time, rather than the spirit's perfect, timeless trance. "Vacillation," of course, as its title indicates, expresses the poet's central inner conflict: he is still, and probably always will be, torn by that old battle between Self and Soul. But in the end he rejects the saintly, spiritual Christian, Von Hügel (stanza 8), asserting that "Homer is my example, and his unchristened heart." Then, in *Words for Music Perhaps*, a long series of marvelous, stripped yet (as Yeats noted in the title) musical lyrics, the poet rises to almost his greatest heights in praise of the body's life and loves. The Crazy Jane poems, of course, are the earthiest and most determinedly physical of these, but they are also profoundly moving in their depiction of "the anguish of mortality," for their praise of the body is presented entirely from the point of view of an aged woman whose dearest one-time lover is long since dead, and who might herself be almost mad with rage and grief and the torment of old memories were she not still so brimful of bitter vitality. Thus, despite age and adversity she rejects the claims of the spirit as practically identical with the feeble hypocritical claims of the established Church (personified as the Bishop, who "has a skin, God knows,/Wrinkled like the foot of a goose.") Indeed, the spirit's existence—Jane asserts—is simply a continuation and intensification of the body's (cf. poem 4, "Crazy Jane and Jack the Journeyman"), and through all the griefs of life the body "makes no moan/But sings on," instinctively aware that "*all things*," even physical things, "*remain in God.*"

Poem 6 of this series—"Crazy Jane Talks with the Bishop"—is central in its presentation of these ideas. Meeting the hypocritical, canting Bishop (her one-time lover, according to Unterecker) on the road, Crazy Jane answers his pious preachings with a declaration of her own profound faith that "Fair and foul are near of kin,/And fair needs foul," explaining further that

> ' . . . Love has pitched his mansion in
> The place of excrement;
> For nothing can be sole or whole
> That has not been rent.'

COMMENT: The puns in these last two lines (sole/Soul, whole/hole) are, of course, obvious. But more important is the large acceptance of life, the reconciliation to the tattered and battered body, interdependence of proud soul and battered body, shining sword and tattered sheath that they imply. This reminds us most strongly of the great hymn of praise with which the "Dialogue of Self and Soul" concludes, of the poet's triumphant assertion there that "Everything we look upon is blessed," no matter how foul or painful, how hideous or humiliating.

The seven earthy Crazy Jane poems are balanced by a more innocent group of love poems ("Girl's Song," "Young Man's Song," etc.) which follow them, and then the entire series is rounded out by a final group of poems in which (except for the Tom-the-Lunatic lyrics) Yeats seems to be speaking primarily in his own *persona*. Of these, poems 17, 18, 19 and 20 are the most moving, with their straightforward, lyrical depiction of the agonies of age. They are brief songs merely, but almost Shakespearian in their terse, half-mad intensity. "Bolt and bar the shutter,/For the foul winds blow," sounds like Tom o' Bedlam on the heath in *King Lear*, as does "Those Dancing Days are Gone:"

> Come, let me sing into your ear;
> Those dancing days are gone,
> All that silk and satin gear;
> Crouch upon a stone,
> Wrapping that foul body up
> In as foul a rag;
> *I carry the sun in a golden cup,*
> *The moon in a silver bag.*

"I am of Ireland," based on a medieval lyric, is one of Yeats' most famous and evocative lyrics of this sort. The repeated "Time runs on" gives it a sense of wild urgency. "The night grows rough" suggests again the Lear-like terrors of wintry storm and wind. The irrational, unexplained setting ("One man alone/In that outlandish gear,/One solitary man/Of all that rambled there"— where? why?) is intriguing, perplexing—and disturbing. Yet the figure of the dancer is, of course, a familiar one, and "the Holy Land of Ireland" reminds us, too, of "the Holy city of Byzantium." Only this time we feel that, amid all the chaos of broken and "accursed" instruments, through all the strange and discordant music, it is life, the life in time, the life of the body—the body of the dancer—that is beckoning, and not, as in "Sailing to Byzantium," pure timelessness. And, indeed, "Tom the Lunatic," in poem 22, speaks for Yeats, declaring the poet's final faith in flesh and blood.

> 'Whatever stands in field or flood,
> Bird, beast, fish or man,
> Mare or stallion, cock or hen,
> Stands in God's unchanging eye
> In all the vigour of its blood;
> In that faith I live or die.'

COMMENT: God's eye, we should notice, is "unchanging," though blood, of course, decays. Thus Yeats does still preserve some balance between time and timelessness, a balance best expressed in the next poem, "Tom at Cruachan" (poem 23), in which the poet asserts, in his most Blakeian style, that "the stallion Eternity/Mounted the mare of Time,/'Gat the foal of the world." Time and eternity, rather than being in conflict, are complementary opposites, on both of which man's world depends for its existence—indeed, for its very genesis. The changeless sword must be encased in the frail silken sheath, the eternal spirit in its battered casing of flesh and blood.

"A Woman Young and Old," the series of eleven poems with which *The Winding Stair* concludes, was deliberately placed at the end of the section to echo and answer the series on "A Man Young and Old" with which *The Tower* closed (if one regards "All Souls' Night" as a kind of epilogue). Like that earlier cycle, this one consists of brief and moving lyrics describing the progress of life and love from youth to age, only this time from the woman's point of view. Poem 10, "Meeting," is perhaps the most poignant, reminding us in its description of the aged lovers—their souls disguised beneath "this beggarly habiliment" of wrinkled flesh—of the fury and pathos of the Crazy Jane series. Like "A Man Young and Old," "A Woman Young and Old" ends with an elegiac translation from the Greek of Sophocles, as if, great poet though he was, Yeats felt so keenly the edge of sorrow which sharpens "short life or long" that he had to go to another poet—an ancient poet—to find properly solemn and time-worn words with which to summarize and conclude the cycle of an individual's experience.

FROM "A FULL MOON IN MARCH"

INTRODUCTION: Yeats himself was dissatisfied with many of the poems in this section. He was in a phase where, his health and strength gradually ebbing away, he felt physically and spiritually sterile. Finally, in desperation, he submitted to the Steinach operation for rejuvenation (through monkey glands), a medical procedure which had gained considerable fame—indeed, notoriety—at the time. Whether, however, for psychological or physical reasons, the operation on Yeats was a great success. The aging poet responded with a tremendous burst of creative energy which lasted from 1934 (the year when the surgery was done) until his death in 1939.

The poems in this section are of three kinds: songs from plays, which tend for the most part to be a bit mechanical and forced; political meditations or songs, which are rather more meaningful;

and metaphysical speculations—the "Supernatural Songs"—which are the book's chief ornaments, most of them written, incidentally, after Yeats' creative energies had been renewed by his operation. In all the poems, however, whether purely musical, personal, political or metaphysical, the tendency of the style is increasingly toward simplicity, toward a return to the stripped precision of *Responsibilities* and *The Green Helmet*. Only now the terse epigrammatic utterances have become almost gnomic, drawn more often from a Blakeian prophetic vein than from the earlier Swiftian vein of savage wit. As Yeats grew older he discarded many of the elaborate esoteric trappings of *A Vision* as he had once (cf. "A Coat") discarded the dreamy, legendary trappings of faeryland with which his earliest poems were laden. Yet, aging into the bare and fierce "desolation of reality," stripping away intricate symbol-systems like a soul discarding excess metaphysical baggage in the preparation for death, Yeats nevertheless could not help but remain under the influence of all those years of occult research. Thus the "Supernatural Songs," the greatest metaphysical utterances of his last years, are marked by terminology from *A Vision* and drenched in esoteric lore—the theories of Hermes Trismegistus ("as above, so below"), the worm Ouroboros, Swedenborgian revelations, etc. Yet, as in *The Winding Stair*, these new visions of eternity only reinforce the poet's sense of its necessary connection with time. It is his old Platonism we see in him, only now without the old longing for the ideal, the old revulsion against the real. Indeed, reality—rage, desolation, sexual passion—at last brings the poet to God, whose self-begetting sexuality—a kind of cosmic conflagration—is simply a higher and fiercer expression of the essential intensity of life, of reality, of generation in time.

POLITICS: The first two poems of this section are, as is obvious, political. The first, "Parnell's Funeral," describes the funeral in 1891 of the Irish leader Parnell. This great Irish hero, who probably did more in the cause of Irish nationalism than any other figure, was rejected by a good portion of his own people when it was revealed that he was living with another man's wife. In "priest-ridden Ireland," divorce, of course, was impossible, and adultery too was a mortal sin (though the lack of divorce made it inevitable). Thus the populace was split into two violently opposed factions by the Parnell case. The more pious Catholics, rejected their one-time hero out of hand, and the less religious patriots remained fiercely loyal. Yeats, who (like Joyce, too—cf. "Ivy Day In the Committee Room," in *Dubliners*, for example) regarded Parnell as a great man, depicted him in "Parnell's Funeral" as a sacrifice to the madness and blood-lust of the mob. Thus the poet's position in this piece is again the old aristocratic one; the common people are vulgar, foolish, bestial; they could only have been ennobled by the great leaders whom their folly leads them to reject. And Parnell, who died bitter and disillusioned almost surely as a result of the way in which he was rejected by the very people to whose freedom he had dedicated his life, is described as having walked "in Jonathan Swift's dark grove, and there/Plucked bitter wisdom that enriched his blood"—that is, as having learned the same terrible truths about mankind's folly and wickedness that drove Swift mad with rage and bitterness two centuries before.

The next poem—a group of three poems actually, "Three Songs to the Same Tune"—is a set of variations on what was originally a marching song written by Yeats for General O'Duffy's "blue-shirt" political movement, a kind of ultra-nationalistic Irish fascist party with which the poet engaged in a mild flirtation for a brief period in the early thirties. After being disillusioned by the movement, however, Yeats revised the lyrics of the three songs, making them wilder and more "fantastical" so that he might not seem to be advocating any particular political course.

METAPHYSICS: Of the poems which intervene between the section's opening political statements and the "Supernatural Songs" which are its climax and conclusion, "A Prayer for Old Age" most movingly expresses Yeats' new faith in passionate reality. But it is in "The Supernatural Songs," as we have already noted, that this faith finds its most brilliant and complex expression. These brief, Blakeian, visionary utterances—some spoken in the *persona* of Ribh, a twelfth century Christian mystic, and some presumably by the poet himself—are among Yeats' finest and most fascinating works. In the first, "Ribh at the Tomb of Baile and Ailinn," the mystic reads his holy book in darkness by the supernatural light of angelic intercourse as Swedenborg described it. Baile and Ailinn, legendary lovers, have become such Swedenborgian angels after death and, Yeats asserts, their earlier human sexuality was but a pale prefiguring of the ecstatic sexual conflagration into which they are assumed after death, the holy sexuality which perpetually begets the world.

> . . . when such bodies join
> There is no touching here, nor touching there,
> Nor straining joy, but whole is joined to whole;
> For the intercourse of angels is a light
> Where for its moment both seem lost, consumed.

In poem 2, "Ribh denounces Patrick," the mystic speaker elaborates further on this idea of divine sexuality.

Natural and supernatural with the self-same ring are wed.
As man, as beast, as an ephemeral fly begets, Godhead
   begets Godhead,
For things below are copies, the Great Smaragdine
   Tablet said.

> **COMMENT:** The Great Smaragdine Tablet bore the
> ancient doctrine of "correspondences" of Hermes Trisme-
> gistus, a pre-Christian Egyptian mystic (or group of mys-
> tics) whose revelations antedated and influenced the Neo-
> platonist doctrines of the Renaissance. Occultists like Yeats
> were, of course, thoroughly familiar with this whole body
> of "Hermetic" work, whose central idea (as stated on
> the Smaragdine or Emerald Tablet) was "as above, so
> below." Things below, that is, in the physical world, are
> but copies of the higher, non-physical reality of the eternal
> world of forms. Thus, Yeats reasons here, if men and beasts
> and even flies are driven into existence by sexuality, God,
> of whom they are but poor copies, must himself be generated
> by a kind of divine sexuality. This description of the sexually
> driven natural world reminds us, of course, of the lines with
> which "Sailing to Byzantium" opens, of "those dying
> generations at their song" of sexuality. But the poet's
> attitude toward this multiplicity of copulation, toward
> "fish, flesh, or fowl . . ." caught up in their sensual begetting,
> seems to have changed greatly. When he wrote the earlier
> poem he felt one must escape into a static eternal shape of
> wisdom. Now he declares that the immortal is just as
> dynamically sexual as the mortal, that "natural and super-
> natural with the self-same ring are wed."

Poem 3 expresses again Ribh's ecstatic perception of the divine
sexuality, and poem 4, "There," describes the mystical place of
union to God, significantly enough in terms of the roaring energy
of the Sun. Yeats, we know, read some of the works of D. H.
Lawrence (who died in 1930) with considerable pleasure, and he
may well have been influenced by the English writer's view of sex
as just such a holy and healing conflagration and of the sun as a
symbol of the divine and vital sexual energy which animates
the universe.

In poem 5, "Ribh Considers Christian Love Insufficient," the
mystic, speaking for the poet, asserts that, divine love being beyond man's mortal capability, only passionate hatred can clear
the soul of petty concerns and prepare it to apprehend the divine
energy and love of God more truly. Thought, too, all the poor
philosophies of man, must be cast away, for "Thought is a

garment and the soul's a bride/That cannot in that trash and tinsel hide." The Soul must rather (continuing the emphasis on sexuality) stand naked at the hour of death—life's "midnight" —before its God. Finally Yeats makes the great religious statement which is at the heart of this poem, his ultimate statement of faith in a God who begets and is begotten by the universe, who animates it and is indeed almost identical with it:

> At stroke of midnight soul cannot endure
> A bodily or mental furniture.
> What can she take until her Master give!
> Where can she look until He make the show!
> What can she know until He bid her know!
> How can she live till in her blood He live!

Poem 6 uses moon-imagery drawn from *A Vision* to express again a mystical perception of sexual identity: "I am I, am I," and poem 7, "What Magic Drum?", seems to be describing, in evocatively sensual terms, the process by which "Godhead on Godhead in sexual passion begot/Godhead." The second stanza, with its incantatory questions, reminds us most strongly of Blake's "Tyger," with its similarly magical reiterated rhetorical questions. Poem 8 again asserts that "Eternity is passion," and poem 9 describes man's wars on God, the furious energy of hatred which prepares the soul for God's victory, as we already saw in poem 5. Poems 10 and 11 are gnomic (enigmatic) visionary utterances, put, especially 10, in terms of *A Vision*.

Poem 12, "Meru," rounds out the poet's vision of desolate reality. Man, though his civilization is based on the "manifold illusion" of great myths, cannot help destroying them with his endlessly questioning, speculative intellect, the "thought" which is of such central importance to his life. And though he is naked and terrified without the protection of his myths, he can never cease "ravening through century after century,/Ravening, raging, and uprooting that he may come/Into the desolation of reality." Thus all his great civilizations are destroyed by the destruction of the myths on which they were based, a truth which the wisest hermits of the Himalayas know perfectly well: the truth that even as night succeeds day, death succeeds life and each civilization obliterates the myths and monuments of the one before. Man, as King Lear saw—and Yeats, as we have noted, has reached the same kind of tragic, half-mad intensity in his own old age— is nothing more than a "poor forked animal," and "winter's dreadful blast" upon the naked bodies of the wise hermits tells them that "before dawn/His glory and his monuments are gone." Thus, as Ribh resolved in poem 5, Yeats also, in his own old age, resolves to cast away all "bodily and mental furniture," the trappings of ancient myth and modern belief, and stand naked at midnight before his God, that he might more readily be assumed into the supernatural conflagration of which natural process is so true a mirror.

LAST POEMS

INTRODUCTION: This final section of Yeats' *Collected Poems* consists of a group of verses published in 1938 as *New Poems*, which were, of course, carefully arranged and organized by the poet, plus another group of poems which were left by him when he died and subsequently set by editors into an order that seemed best to approximate the order he himself would have chosen. The mood of the poems, however, is fairly consistent throughout. It is the mood of life acceptance, of affirmation of reality, that informed *"From A Full Moon in March"* too, the mood of tragic gaiety—dynamic, exultant in the face of desolation—which gave a new and wild strength to the aging poet's work.

Amid all this exultation and acceptance, however, it is important to note that the poet's affirmation was purely metaphysical; it did not extend itself (as it did not in *"A Full Moon"* either) to the political-historical sphere of events. If anything, Yeats became more aristocratic and less conventionally democratic as he grew older, increasingly certain that a great society must be led by a trained and superior nobility, though rooted in the legends and labor of the people. For the timid "merchant and the clerk"— the hypocritical, materialistic, unimaginative middle-class—there is, at any rate, no room, of this he was sure. Thus in his political poems (of which there are quite a few in this section) he praised the proud and hard-riding aristocratics, the horsemen of Ben Bulben and the leaders of Dublin (both groups being not necessarily "noble" by birth but noble in the truest sense, by nature). He praised the folk, the peasants and the beggars, too. But modern civilization, with its democratic middle-class majority, he saw as coming at the end, the "black out" of an historical "gyre."

Folk themes, however, are of more than political importance in this volume. Yeats kept his copy of the Oxford Book of Ballads —a gift from Dorothy Wellesley, an important new literary friend —at his bedside in these years, and his use of the ballad form and of ballad-like refrains as intensifiers even in nonballads was one of the more significant ways in which his final style evolved. He was already, of course, writing stripped, intense, succinct poems, both narrative and speculative (cf. *Words for Music Perhaps* and "Supernatural Songs"), but the ballads and ballad-like lyrics in

Last Poems have a more traditional quality that was lacking in the earlier poems. It almost seems as though Yeats, in some of his late ballads—like "The O'Rahilly," "That Wild Old Wicked Man," "The Statesman's Holiday" and "John Kinsella's Lament for Mrs. Mary Moore"—had come full circle, back to the ballad forms of his most youthful volumes (cf. e.g. "The Ballad of the Foxhunter," with which *Crossways* closes). But where the earlier poems had been faintly literary, derivative, pretentious, these new ones were taut with genuine emotion, rich with the accumulated experience of fifty years. All that had intervened—the anguish of hopeless love, the careful esoteric system of *A Vision*, the final release of sexual and religious energies, the political events and activities, the marriage, the children, the success—all helped to shape these ballads, like Yeats' other last poems, into a true and final expression of the poet's mature genius.

TRAGIC GAIETY: Tragic gaiety—the gaiety of heroes, who respond to the "desolation of reality" with courageous laughter, who meet death with a defiant smile—is the prevailing mood of most of Yeats' last poems. But the first poems in the section especially "The Gyres" and "Lapis Lazuli," express this mood most fully and frankly. Both works deal with Yeats' old subject, history, and with the chaos of both the present and the past, the chaos of shifting historical cycles or "gyres." But Yeats' final response to this chaos is no longer the horror he expressed in "Nineteen Hundred and Nineteen," "I See Phantoms" (cf. "Meditations in Time of Civil War") and "The Second Coming." Now—as befits a poet who reconciled himself to all things, indeed blessed them, in *The Winding Stair* (cf. especially "A Dialogue of Self and Soul")—he accepts the pain of history with "tragic joy" (stanzas 1 and 2 of "The Gyres").

> What matter though numb nightmare ride on top,
> And blood and mire the sensitive body stain?
> What matter? Heave no sigh, let no tear drop,
> A greater, a more gracious time has gone;
> For painted forms or boxes of make-up
> In ancient tombs I sighed, but not again;
> What matter? Out of cavern came a voice,
> And all it knows is that one word 'Rejoice!'

And in stanza 3 of "The Gyres" the poet adds that, in any case, the old "unfashionable gyre" of the past—in this case the cycle of history dominated by workman, noble and saint (probably the Middle Ages, of which Yeats was an admirer)—will at any rate come round again, in due course.

COMMENT: The phrase "old Rocky Face" has given many critics much trouble. This Face, which the poet addresses in line 1 of stanza 1 and which is described in line 2 of stanza 2 as holding "dear" all "lovers of horses and of women" (and which is probably meant also as the source of the caverned voice which in stanza 2 bids the poet to "Rejoice"), has been identified variously as the Delphic Oracle, the Rocky Voice "in a cleft that's christened Alt" (cf. "The Man and the Echo") and the face of the moon. Probably another—perhaps the best—possibility would be to identify the Rocky Face with the mountainous rocky face of the earth itself, and the later Rocky Voice as earth's voice. Certainly both "The Gyres" and the later "The Man and the Echo" are full enough of caverns, clefts, broken stones, marble and ancient tombs to suggest the rocky, intransigent surface of the earth. And the description of the spirit which informs both face and voice—holding dear the vital and dynamic (lovers of horses and women, natural aristocrats), bidding "Rejoice!"—seems indeed a kind of earth spirit, a kind of life principle which unites life's joy, its animation, with its tragedy, its stony desolation.

In "Lapis Lazuli" Yeats elaborates this idea of tragic joy, expressing it, finally, in a new and more specific set of symbols. In stanza 1 he describes the reaction of certain "hysterical women" to art. They are "tired" of the artist's gaiety, for it does nothing "drastic" to alleviate the world-situation. In stanza 2, however, the poet asserts that "all perform their tragic play" and there is gaiety in the performance. That is, that unlike hysterical women, who "break up their lines to weep," heroes like Hamlet and Lear are "gay,/Gaiety transfiguring all that dread," and artists, whom the women think superfluous, know this. (Many such connectives in the poem—that is, the ideas which link one stanza to the next —are implicit, left to the critic or reader to supply for himself.) Stanza 3 deals with the same historical material as "The Gyres." "They" refers to the "old civilizations put to the sword" by time. Yet though "all things fall and are built again," the poet accepts the cycles of history with "tragic joy," asserting that "those that build them again are gay." In stanzas 4 and 5 Yeats crystallizes this idea of tragic gaiety in the image of three Chinamen carved on a lump of lapis lazuli that was given him by Harry Clifton. The three old men are pictured in the stone as climbing toward a "little half-way house," sweetened, the poet supposes, by "plum or cherry-branch." Then he imagines that seated there, "on all the tragic scene they stare."

> One asks for mournful melodies;
> Accomplished fingers begin to play.
> Their eyes mid many wrinkles, their eyes,
> Their ancient, glittering eyes, are gay.

Their gaiety is a result, not only of their ancient wisdom, which profoundly comprehends "the tragic scene," but also of the "mournful melodies" played by the "accomplished fingers" of the artist ("doubtless a serving man"), music which enables both him and his listeners to transfigure "all that dread." For art—the often cryptic, yet always meaningful carvings in the stone, the lapis lazuli, of time—no matter how tragic, how "mournful," transfigures all tragedy with the doomed defiant gaiety of the hero and the sage, the wiseman and the fool. Indeed, it is from these last apparent yet complementary opposites that the hysterical majority—the nervous and vulgar mass of middle-brow matrons, merchants and clerks—must learn to live with the old style, the old audacity, the old nobility.

> **COMMENT:**   It is interesting to notice the prevalence of stone imagery in many of Yeats' last poems. In connection with "The Gyres" we discussed the significance of "old Rocky Face," who will later, we noted, reappear as a Rocky Voice, in "The Man and the Echo." Here the three wise Chinamen are carved in stone, in lapis lazuli, which suggested to Yeats—as he wrote to Dorothy Wellesley— "Ascetic, pupil, hard stone, eternal theme of the sensual east. The heroic cry in the midst of despair." And, indeed, in most of these poems stone seems to serve a double purpose, to represent both the hard—often bitter—intransigence of fate, the harshness of *things*, the "desolation of reality" (this because it is sterile, non-living, compared, say, to trees, which represent life and fertility), and also, at the same time, eternity, the eternity of truth, of the forms of life and of art, which abides unchanged through all the "gyres" and cycles of man's history as the earth abides unchanged through all man's changing days upon it.

"Imitated From the Japanese," whose meaning is clear and obvious, and "Sweet Dancer" round out this first group of poems devoted to tragic gaiety. "Sweet Dancer" reintroduces one of Yeats' oldest and most central symbols, the dancer who, in this case, is so caught up in her dance—her art—that she can momentarily escape "from bitter youth," from the "black cloud" of reality. Thus hers, like the Chinese musicians', is the tragic gaiety which defies desolation by creating a new and sweeter world of its own. Though this particular poem was probably inspired by Yeats' relationship with a mad girl, Margot Ruddock, who actually did escape from reality by doing such a dance on the beach near his house, we certainly do not need to know the biographical details in order to appreciate this lyric with its poignant refrain—"*Ah, dancer, ah, sweet dancer!*"—in and of itself.

BALLAD AND AUTOBIOGRAPHY: The majority of the poems in this section, as we have already noted, are either ballads, often with political or philosophical overtones, or more personal, subjective works in Yeats' famous autobiographical vein—poems of reminiscence, reflection, confession. The series entitled "The Three Bushes" tells the story of a high-born lady who, wanting both to keep her own chastity and to satisfy her lover, hits on the idea of having her chambermaid take her place in bed at night. Within the framework of this story (which reminds us vaguely of the early "Anashuya and Vijaya"—cf. Yeats' note to *Crossways*), the poet explores the relationship between body and soul—their inescapable interdependence—and between love and pleasure. Then, in "An Acre of Grass" and "What Then?" he turns to more immediately personal concerns, expressing his impatience, "here at life's end," with all that he has so far achieved. "Grant me an old man's frenzy," he begs in "An Acre of Grass," for he would still pierce the clouds of existence and find the truth beyond. Despite all his success, he admits, in the insistent refrain of "What Then?," he still is urged forward by the ceaseless questioning of "Plato's ghost," of the eternally dissatisfied spirit of man's intellect, which always wants to know "What then?" What are the final discoveries, the ultimate achievements— mysteries unravelled, truths perceived—which will follow worldly and artistic success?

In the next three poems Yeats celebrates his old friends and new protégées. "Beautiful Lofty Things" praises the arrogant courage, the nobility, indeed the heroism of his oldest associates—O'Leary, his father, Standish O'Grady, Augusta Gregory, Maud Gonne. "A Crazed Girl" deals with the same Margot Ruddock who inspired "Sweet Dancer," and "To Dorothy Wellesley" is addressed to the literary protégée who helped enliven his last years with her insistent intellectual attentions.

COMMENT: Yeats' admiration for Dorothy Wellesley ("What climbs the stair?/Nothing that common women ponder on/If you are worthy my hope!") reminds us in a way of his similar feeling for Augusta Gregory (which was enriched by his gratitude to her as a friend and patroness, however). It seems as though we can detect two attitudes toward women in the poet. One feeling he has, as we know, is that beautiful women should not be intellectual, and especially not political. They should simply be gracious and beautiful, for the genius of their bodies is greater than anything their minds can do. Thus, by extension, they become symbols of the body's wisdom (cf. "Michael Robartes and the Dancer") and of the beauty of tradition (cf. "A Prayer for My Daughter" and "In Memory of Eva Gore-Booth and Con Markiewicz"). On the other hand, Yeats certainly never dismisses women as inherently men's intellectual inferiors. They can be quite as proud, as noble, as heroic, as wise. Thus Augusta Gregory and Maud Gonne are grouped with O'Leary and O'Grady as "beautiful" and "lofty" things, and Dorothy Wellesley is visited by "the Proud Furies, each with her torch on high."

"The Curse of Cromwell," "Roger Casement" and "The Ghost of Roger Casement," "The O'Rahilly" and "Come Gather Round Me Parnellites" are all political ballads. The first denounces Cromwell's "murderous crew" and, by extension, the mercantile middle class whom Cromwell represents, for they are responsible for destroying the old, brave, proud, aristocratic order whose passing the poet mourns. The other ballads are all nationalistic pieces which deal with various heroes of the Irish struggle for independence, with Roger Casement, O'Rahilly and, of course, Charles Stewart Parnell, the by now almost legendary leader who was also the subject of the earlier "Parnell's Funeral."

"The Wild Old Wicked Man," last of this group of poems, deals with old age again, only in more general terms than "An Acre of Grass" and "What Then?" "The wild old man," who celebrates the vivid fury of reality, rejects a spiritual lady, who has given all her love to God ("that old man in the skies") and rejects spirituality in general in favor of "the second-best," life's earthy pleasures. Yet—a kind of "Mask" for Yeats in his old age—this wild old man is not wholly physical in his talents. Wild as he is, he has an almost supernatural wisdom to match his wildness—"Words I have that can pierce the heart," the poet's genius—and

'A young man in the dark am I,
But a wild old man in the light,
That can make a cat laugh, or
Can touch by motherwit
Things hid in their marrow-bones
From time long passed away,
Hid from all those warty lads
That by their bodies lay.'

COMMENT: Imbued with an urgency and intensity, a wildness that is obviously personal, this simple, straightforward yet fiercely imagined poem is one of the best in this section. Its refrain—"Daybreak and a candle-end"—suggests the wearing down of the old man's life, the (paradoxical) dawning of death upon the long passionate night of his life, the night in which he so often forgot the pain of things awhile "upon a woman's breast." But the light—daybreak—suggests revelation, too, the revelation that has come with age ("A young man in the dark am I,/But a wild old man in the light,/That can make a cat laugh," etc.) And the first lines of the poem—"Because I am mad about women,/I am mad about the hills," remind us simultaneously of the earth's rejoicing rocky face with which this section opened (cf. "The Gyres"), of the earth's voluptuous configurations, and of the exultation of the beggarmen in *Responsibilities* who, freed of conventional restraints, were "Running to Paradise." More, these lines, like the poem's refrain, have that touch of the inexplicable, that touch of truth unsayable in any other way, that is, too, the touch of genius, the mark of a great poem.

BALLADS AND EPIGRAMS: Ballads, ballads and more ballads are the stuff of *Last Poems*, but the volume also includes a number of epigrams in the old, terse, bitter style. "The Great Day," "Parnell" and "What Was Lost" are political, expressing Yeats' longstanding disenchantment with "the people" and with the chaos of the new century. "The Spur" is personal, and in four lines it expresses what was also the central idea of "The Wild Old Wicked Man." "A Drunken Man's Praise of Sobriety," with its implicit praise of drunkenness and dancing, reminds us of the early "Fiddler of Dooney," where folk danced "like a wave of the sea," as they do here. Even in those days, indeed, Yeats could celebrate the tragic gaiety of the dancer, caught up in the merry exaltation of natural rhythm, yet "under every dancer/A dead man in his grave." "The Pilgrim" and "Colonel Martin" are two more exercises in the ballad form. And finally, "A Model for the Laureate" and "The Old Stone Cross" are political reflections cast in rather ballad-like shapes, mainly because of their use of ballad meter (4343, etc.) and ballad refrains.

IMAGES OF THE PAST: The next few poems deal, as did "Beautiful Lofty Things," with Yeats' memories of his past life, his reminiscences of his oldest (and noblest) friends, and of his long devotion to art. The first two, "The Spirit Medium" and "Those Images," are speculations about the relationship between art and life. In the end, the poet concludes (drawing an image from Plato), one should leave "the cavern of the mind" and "recognize the five" (the five senses) "that make the Muses sing" —that is, he asserts, art is dependent on physical reality for its imagery and inspiration.

Then, in "The Municipal Gallery Revisited," a superb, intricately structured yet conversational poem along the lines of "In Memory of Major Robert Gregory," Yeats takes an imaginary tour of the Dublin gallery where hang portraits of his oldest friends—Augusta Gregory, John Synge, Robert Gregory, Hugh Lane—and of Ireland's greatest leaders—Griffith, O'Higgins, etc.—looking not as they were, but as they are in art, in spirit, "terrible and gay." But as he walks about, recalling the past, the poet succumbs to nostalgia and despair, for looking upon these "permanent and impermanent images of his life," he fears "that time may bring/ Approved patterns of women or of men/But not that selfsame excellence again." Finally, in "Are You Content?" the poet expresses the mood of "What Then?" Addressing—and recalling —his most notable ancestors (as he did in "Pardon, old fathers," at the beginning of *Responsibilities*), he declares that he is not yet content with his work, not yet, in other words, ready to retire to a secluded spot where he "might stay/In some good company . . . smiling at the sea."

POLITICAL AND METAPHYSICAL: "Three Songs to the One Burden," more political ballads really, denounce again the chaos and commonness of modern times, and praise the heroism of the past. The stirring refrain which links all three—"*From mountain to mountain ride the fierce horsemen*"—provides important background material that will later help us understand "Under Ben Bulben," Yeats' great poetic "last will and testament," when we come to it. "The fierce horsemen" here are the "men that ride upon horses" whom we first encountered in "At Galway Races," and who are almost always symbols of heroic aristocracy for Yeats. Here they are riding through the mountains, presumably rousing a brave band which will soon come to overthrow the dull and common democratic cycle of modern history and set things "on that unfashionable gyre" of the past—"the workmen, noble and saint"—again.

Where the "Three Songs" were political in subject, "In Tara's Halls," "The Statues" and "News for the Delphic Oracle" are metaphysical exercises of Yeats' speculative imagination. The first expresses the heroic idea that things should be done for their own sake, courageously and gaily. "God I have loved," the "praiseworthy man" asserts, "but should I ask return/Of God or woman, the time were come to die." The second—"The Statues" —through complex historical images (Pythagoras, Hamlet, Buddha, Cuchulain, all of whom are used symbolically, of course) describes the evolution of modern times and the relationship, through history, of the real and the ideal. The boys and girls of stanza 1, who press "live lips upon a plummet-measured [abstractly perfect] face"—embracing the ideal—in doing so help to make it real ("passion can bring character enough."). And in stanza 4 Yeats suggests that all heroism is based on such a relationship of the real and the ideal, of Pearse (real) and Cuchulain (ideal). Thus the Irish, who were "born into that ancient sect" of the ideally heroic but have now been "thrown upon this filthy modern tide," should "climb to our proper dark," the midnight dark where the boys and girls of stanza 1 publicly embrace statues of perfection, "that we may trace/The lineaments of a plummet-measured face."

In "News for the Delphic Oracle," the third of these metaphysical speculations, Yeats analyzes the relationship between spirituality and sexuality. The "News" that even after death, after they have crossed the waters of what in "Byzantium" was described as "that dolphin-torn, that gong-tormented sea," the "Innocents" "copulate in the foam" to "the intolerable music" of Pan, reminds us of the sexual conflagration of Baile and Ailinn in "Supernatural Songs." Here, however, the sexuality is brutal, intolerable, whereas there it was mystical, luminous. Reality—even the "reality" of the after-life—becomes in *Last Poems* ever more physical, sensual, desolate. Yet the physical is paradoxically intertwined with the spiritual, and the desolate, as we have seen, with the tragically gay.

"Three Marching Songs," returning to politics, are simply earlier versions of the "Three Songs to the Same Tune" which appeared in *A Full Moon*. The "Long Legged Fly," on the other hand, is one of Yeats' finest speculations on the nature of power, a subject which always fascinated him (cf. "A Woman Homer Sung" and "Leda and the Swan," among others). Thus it unites politics and metaphysics in its vivid, evocative descriptions of Caesar, Helen and Michelangelo, who represent political, sensual and artistic power, and each of whose minds strangely, inexplicably, "moves upon silence/Like a long-legged fly upon the stream." The nature of the uncommon, the extraordinary individual, is fascinating and incomprehensible: his mind is always moving, yet gently, easily, its power leashed. Moving thus it mysteriously skims the surface of the unknown, of "silence," as lightly and mysteriously as a long-legged fly maintains itself upon the surface of a stream without drowning or flying away.

> **COMMENT:**   This refrain is a particularly successful one, and one which finally defies analysis, reminding us in its really inexplicable vividness of the refrain of "The Wild Old Wicked Man" and some of Yeats' other successful refrains. Indeed, it is the function of the refrain in most of these poems not only, as in traditional ballads, to link the various verses of the piece together, to unify the poem, but also, as it were, to summarize the poem in a single image or statement, usually more obscure because more concentrated and intense than the rest of the work. Thus the refrain is frequently the most evocative line in the poem, the one that sets the mood. And, in the end, a brilliant refrain like the one in "Long Legged Fly," proves that Yeats belongs in the very company he describes, for his own mind, too—with its power to create such a line—moves, as did Michelangelo's, over the silent, mysterious surface of things "like a long-legged fly upon the stream."

PERSONAL LEGENDS: In the final sixteen poems of this section Yeats deals with what we might call personal legends, with a kind of compendium of his oldest and dearest themes. As John Unterecker has noted, in preparing himself for death the poet probably felt he ought to review the images and ideas out of which he made the art of a lifetime. The first of the poems in this group is, fittingly enough, about Maud Gonne, about a bronze head of the aged woman his once beautiful beloved has become. Though now, as she is shown in the statue, she is all "withered and mummy-dead" except for her almost supernaturally keen eyes, the poet can remember when her form was "all full/As though with magnanimity of light." Remembering, he reviews the ways in which he had imagined her—both as a real, a natural person, full of wildness and terror, and as a kind of supernatural creature, a Platonic ideal of visionary wisdom (cf. Introduction to *The Wind Among the Reeds*), who seemed to be staring disapprovingly at modern times, "as though a sterner eye looked through her eye/On this foul world in its decline and fall."

"A Stick of Incense" deals in Yeats' old epigrammatic way with the Christian myth, while "John Kinsella's Lament for Mrs. Mary Moore" presents, in the course of the lover's lament for his mistress, a happier version of the relationship between aged lovers than Yeats has given us before. In "Meeting," we must remember (poem 10 of "A Woman Young and Old") and in the last few poems of "A Man Young and Old" the lovers grown old were full of hate; they resented and reproached each other for the "beggarly habiliment" in which they found themselves. Now, though, reconciled to age—accepting, indeed, the "desolation of reality" with a new, if tragic, gaiety—Yeats, in the person of the old lover, laments:

> And O! but she had stories,
>   Though not for the priest's ear,
> To keep the soul of man alive,
>   Banish age and care,
> And being old she put a skin
>   On everything she said.
> *What shall I do for pretty girls*
> *Now my old bawd is dead?*

In "Hound Voice" and "Three Songs to the One Burden," Yeats writes again on the theme of the natural aristocracy, those who "love bare hills and stunted trees/And were the last to choose the settled ground,/Its boredom of the desk or of the spade." These lonely courageous individuals he identifies with hounds, "because/So many years companioned by a hound" and because they spoke with the strength and the instinctive blood-wisdom of hounds (cf. also "The Ballad of the Foxhunter," in *Crossways*). "High Talk," on the other hand, is about art, only unlike Yeats' earlier poems about art—e.g., "Sailing to Byzantium" and "Byzantium"—it presents the artist not as an almost supernatural figure, a holy craftsman or seer, but as a kind of trickster, an acrobat who walks on stilts, the highest he can find ("What if my great granddad had a pair that were twenty feet high,/And mine were but fifteen foot, no modern stalks upon higher"). Wild and untamed as a barnacle goose who races out into the light at daybreak, the poet tells us that "I, through the terrible novelty of light, stalk on, stalk on." The poet soars like the goose (birds, we should remember, are almost always symbols of the soaring spirit for Yeats) toward a final revelation, a luminous shore where "those great sea-horses bare their teeth, and laugh at the dawn."

    COMMENT: "Those great sea-horses" are probably an image of the incoming waves which have always seemed to poets to pound the beach like galloping horses with manes of foam flung back, though perhaps they may also be a reference to the dolphins which, in "Byzantium" and "News for the Delphic Oracle," ferry souls to paradise. In any case, they are a good example of the kind of unlocated, essentially indefinable, symbolist image Yeats had been using almost all his life. Interestingly enough, these images, these mysterious symbols, often used the sea or sea-related creatures as vessels into which to pour mysterious significance. "Who Goes With Fergus?" which concludes with a strange vision of "the white breast of the dim sea/And all dissheveled wandering stars" was one of the first poems to use such imagery. And here, though the sea where great horses gallop is probably the sea of the unknown—the unknown which "Malachi Stilt-Jack," poet, prophet and trickster, alone can penetrate—it has still more connotations and elusive meanings than criticism can completely identify.

According to T. R. Henn, "The Apparitions" is a poem about Yeats' increasing—and, of course, very natural—fear of death, a fear which haunted his dreams as well as many of his waking moments. The worst of the dreams—in which he seems to have seen fifteen terrible apparitions—was one in which he saw his empty coat hanging upon a hanger, a vision which symbolized the real physical world as it would, indifferently, continue to exist after he was gone. "A Nativity" is another epigrammatic and rather obscure poem about Yeats' favorite historical subject, the annunciation with which a new historical cycle begins. Here, however, he considers the relationship between art (represented by such artists as the painter Delacroix, the poet Walter Savage Landor, and the actor Henry Irving) and the annunciation, and thus, more generally, between art and history. "Why Should Not Old Men Be Mad?" is simple but intense; it deals with the rage experience brings, the fury of disillusionment, the despair of time. "Young men know nothing of this sort,/Observant old men know it well," the poet declares.

"The Statesman's Holiday," both because of its subject and its musical, stripped vitality, reminds us of "The Wild Old Wicked Man." Like the earlier "Running to Paradise" (*Responsibilities*), it is about a vagabond who rejects the rewards and burdens of conventional society, though, in this case, the speaker already had attained a considerable position in the world. Like "The Fiddler of Dooney," this "irresponsible" fellow becomes an artist, a musician, and he pleases a rejoicing crowd (of "boys and girls around him"). And like many of the figures in Yeats' early, late and middle poems (cf. "The Happy Townland" for instance), this singer's songs are all of a kind of Eden, an eternal paradise, a Happy Land. *"Tall dames go walking in grass-green Avalon"* is the sweet refrain he sings, to all who will listen.

"Crazy Jane on the Mountain" brings back Yeats' earthy favorite, this time on a new subject. "Tired of cursing the Bishop," the mad old woman has "found something worse to meditate on"—the disloyalty of King George V to his "beautiful cousins," the Russian Royal Family, who were "battered to death in a cellar" while "he stuck to his throne." Like Yeats, disgusted with the modern world, Crazy Jane dreams of the noble violence of the legendary heroes of the past, of Cuchulain and his spouse, "great-bladdered Emer," (her great bladder is a sign of her almost supernatural spirit and power).

"THE CIRCUS ANIMALS' DESERTION":   In one of the most famous of his last poems, Yeats consciously reviews the progress of his artistic career. In Section 1 he introduces his present problem. "Being but a broken man," old and weary, he seeks a theme in vain, although he was never troubled in the past by such artistic sterility. Then the images, ideas and themes—like circus animals—came thick and fast, and they "were all on show."

In section 2 Yeats enumerates his own themes. Stanza 1 describes his earliest concern—the Irish faeryland of Oisin, the dreamy vision of the ideal that so preoccupied him in his first volumes. Stanza 2 describes his increasing political involvement and his love for Maud Gonne, two passions which had all his "thought and love" in middle years. Stanza 3 describes the "heart-mysteries" of the symbolist theatre which engrossed him next, and perhaps, by implication, the "heart-mysteries" of *A Vision*, which was so important to him, too. And yet, Yeats admits, basically it was the shine and tinsel of his symbols that attracted him, the "players and painted stage . . . And not those things that they were emblems of."

In section 3 Yeats, as he did so many years earlier in "A Coat," impatiently casts off all his old symbols, all those old trappings and embroideries which gave him metaphors for poetry for so many years. Like the hermits of "Meru," he has come at last into "the desolation of reality." As in "A Coat," he is walking naked again. Pure emotion—or, we should say impure emotion—the base, the bare, the desolate tangle of feelings and ideas which clutter the heart; the passions, fair and foul together (cf. "Crazy Jane Talks To the Bishop")—these are the stuff of poetry, the poet declares, and out of these all the "masterful images" of art are born, though they grow "in pure mind." And now that his "ladder" of themes and tricks is gone, Yeats concludes, he must write of nothing but such emotional reality: "I must lie down where all the ladders start,/In the foul rag-and-bone shop of the heart."

COMMENT: Like Coleridge's "Dejection: An Ode," "The Circus Animals' Desertion" is a great poem about not being able to write poetry. As in the earlier work, the poet moves from a complaint of sterility to some comment on his poetic career (though Coleridge was much less specific than Yeats) to a final declaration of faith both in art and in life—in art's ability to transcend desolate reality and in life's ability to sustain art in its passionate flight. Like Yeats, Coleridge concluded that "from the soul itself must there be sent/A sweet and potent voice, of its own birth,/Of all sweet sounds the life and element!" and that this would wonderfully provide the creative joy that inspires art:

> Joy is the sweet voice, Joy the luminous cloud—
>   We in ourselves rejoice!
> And thence flows all that charms or ear or sight,
>   All melodies the echoes of that voice,
> All colors a suffusion from that light.

And Yeats in "The Circus Animals' Desertion," was really writing about the same thing, about what he earlier called "tragic joy," the heroic gaiety which enables the artist to laugh and sing in the face of desolation or even of death itself.

"Politics" is a witty, epigrammatic poem about youth and age, love and wisdom, whose succinct charm reminds us of the earlier "For Anne Gregory" or "The Scholars." "The Man and the Echo," which was partly discussed earlier (cf. "The Gyres"), puts Yeats' self-doubts and self-questionings in dialogue form. Conscience-ridden, wondering to what extent he is responsible for various political and personal tragedies (reminding us of his state of mind in "At Algeciras: A Meditation Upon Death"), the poet finally succumbs to fears and forebodings.

>   O Rocky Voice,
> Shall we in that great night rejoice?
> What do we know but that we face
> One another in this place?
> But hush, for I have lost the theme,
> Its joy or night seem but a dream;
> Up there some hawk or owl has struck,
> Dropping out of sky or rock,
> A stricken rabbit is crying out,
> And its cry distracts my thought.

"Cuchulain Comforted," written in Dantesque *terza rima*, deals with the process of the after life in terms of what we might call the death and transfiguration of Yeats' favorite hero, Cuchulain (cf. the section on Yeats' "Cuchulain Plays"). "The Black Tower," Yeats' very last poem—dictated to his wife a few days before his death—is a wonderfully harsh, grim picture of the tomb, prophetically death-drenched and ominous. Though long dead, the brave soldiers of the old black tower still stand on guard "oath-bound." Ghosts or old bones standing "upright" in their tombs, they keep out the banners of corruption, adhering to the nobler standards of the past. Though "the dark grows blacker" in their tombs, the poet implies, their day—their gyre—may come again.

"UNDER BEN BULBEN":   This most famous of Yeats' *Last Poems* was completed in September 1938, five months before the poet's death, and in it the poet—uniting his political, metaphysical and aesthetic interests—expresses, as it were, his final view of things, his last word on life and death. Section 1 "sets the scene" with a descriptive evocation of the occult knowledge of all the ages, of both the Egyptian sages of the Mareotic Lake (a reference to Shelley's "Witch of Atlas") and of the supernatural aristocratic horsemen of the Irish mountains (cf. "Three Songs to the One Burden"—"*From mountain to mountain ride the fierce horsemen*"). Section 2 expounds, for the last time, Yeats' cyclical theory of history, which is importantly related to his idea of the soul's immortality through reincarnation. The "two eternities" complement each other: as the soul "gyres" upward toward spiritual perfection through a winding series of ages and incarnations, the race evolves through a series of contrasting historical "gyres" or cycles to *its* final destiny. Thus

> Though grave-diggers' toil is long,
> Sharp their spades, their muscles strong,
> They but thrust their buried men
> Back in the human mind again.

Section 3 outlines the paradoxical concept of healing hatred which was earlier dealt with, at least in part, in "Ribh Considers Christian Love Insufficient." Hatred—violence, really—helps a man to "accomplish fate" and to clear his heart, leaving him at last heroically gay, able to "laugh aloud, his heart at peace." Thus, too, the artist is prepared for his historically inevitable work, work which is dealt with more closely in section 4. In the artist the "two eternities" of race and soul, the two occupations of politics and mysticism, merge in a kind of mystical politics, for it is the job of the artist through all the ups and downs of history, through all the gyres, to "bring the soul of man to God." Thus "measurement"—the abstract system of Pythagoras, for instance—began man's intellectual "might," and "Michelangelo left a proof/On the Sistine Chapel roof." Yet ultimately art—though rooted in the abstract—is concrete, so concrete, indeed, that Michelangelo's "proof," his Adam, can arouse "globe-trotting Madam,/ Till her bowels are in heat." Indeed, it is the "profane perfection of mankind"—the reality of the body as well as the soul (cf. "A Dialogue of Self and Soul") which is the true subject of art. Thus in the painted gardens of the Renaissance the real and the ideal seem to merge, and even after western civilization had declined from that peak ("Gyres run on"), "Calvert and Wilson, Blake and Claude/Prepared a rest for the people of God" (in the words of the visionary nineteenth-century painter Samuel Palmer). Only amid the chaos of modern times, has "confusion" fallen "upon our thought." And in section 5 Yeats tells the Irish poets who will come after him how to deal with this modern confusion.

> . . . learn your trade,
> Sing whatever is well made,
> Scorn the sort now growing up
> All out of shape from toe to top,
> Their unremembering hearts and heads
> Base-born products of base beds.

Art must be, in other words, both shapely and aristocratic, and if artists adhere to these precepts, Yeats asserts, "we in coming days may be/Still the indomitable Irishry."

Section 6 finally, in ringing, dramatic tones, sets forth Yeats' epitaph. The circumstantiality ("in Drumcliff churchyard Yeats is laid,/An ancestor was rector there/Long years ago, a church stands near"), the terseness and simplicity of the whole stanza remind us of "To Be Carved on a Stone at Thoor Ballylee." Indeed, the epitaph itself, which was actually used on the poet's grave, is just the right length for carving in stone.

> *Cast a cold eye*
> *On life, on death.*
> *Horseman, pass by!*

Yeats knew what kind of words should be carved in stone just as he knew what words should be written on paper. A craftsman from first to last, at the end as at the beginning he knew his trade.

COMMENT: The horseman referred to here is one of the riders of stanza one, one of that immortal "pale, long-visaged company," and one of the fierce horsemen of "Three

Songs to the One Burden." He represents, too, the soul, coldly set upon its furious, rushing journey through time, its ascent from chaos to breathless eternity, for what is the soul if not an insubstantial rider in the saddle of substantial flesh? Finally, mystical in concept yet drawn from a political vocabulary (cf., for instance, the horsemen of "At Galway Races"), this great last image unites Yeats' long concern with both these subjects into the elaborately unified system of mystical politics, the symbol-system of history, which he had been constructing all his life, and of which we spoke earlier. And yet, despite all these overtones, all these possible "definitions," this image of the proud and cold-eyed arrogant horseman, is finally greater and more mysterious than any explanation criticism can offer. It depends for its effect on the whole complex of the poem's devices—its meter, its rhyme, its imperative simplicity, the different stanzas and sections which have led up to and prepared the way for it. It is the quality of great art, after all, to be—as we have seen—greater than the sum of its parts, just as the pattern of fifty-nine swans at Coole transcended the fifty-nine individual swans, just as the chestnut tree was more than the leaf, the blossom or the bole, and just as the horseman—the soul of man, the soul of the poet—journeying eternally on, contains, expresses and transcends both life and death and all the shadowy realm between.

YEATS' "CUCHULAIN PLAYS":
SUMMARY AND COMMENT

YEATS' PLAYS: In the course of his long and quite successful career as a playwright, Yeats wrote a great number of plays, including works on Irish, Christian and esoteric themes. It would be impossible, in a book of this length, to deal adequately with all these often complicated and obscure dramas, so emphasis will be placed on what is perhaps the poet's most important contribution to the dramatic form—his elaborate and often brilliant cycle of plays dealing with the legendary Irish hero, Cuchulain of Muirthemne. Peter Ure, probably the best critic to date of Yeats' plays, has pointed out that "the Cuchulain theme had perhaps a more enduring influence on the poetry [and thus, also, the plays] of Yeats than any other Irish mythological subject." And indeed, although Yeats was concerned, as we have seen, with all of the Irish heritage, and often dealt—in both plays and poems— with such figures as Deirdre, Fergus and Oisin, Cuchulain more than any other seems to have served mystical and personal as well as as nationalistic purposes. He was, among other things, a symbol of the Irish Renaissance, an incarnation of all heroic ideals, and a kind of *persona* for the poet's own soul. Almost every phase of his existence fascinated Yeats, and each was dealt with in the cycle of plays built around him, a cycle, incidentally, which spanned the writer's entire dramatic career and may be taken as perfectly representative of his evolution as one of our century's most significant "avant-garde" playwrights.

CUCHULAIN: The "original" of Yeats' Cuchulain was a small, gay, wrathful man, one of the principal heroes of the Ulster or Red-Branch saga. As leader of the Ulstermen and son of a supernatural being, he occupied the place of a kind of Hercules in Irish mythology. In the old legends his adventures are related in a frank and uncomplicated folk style. In 1902, however, Lady Gregory collected all the old tales and retold them in her book *Cuchulain of Muirthemne.* Yeats relied almost entirely on this more sophisticated version of Cuchulain's story for the larger outlines of his work, but constantly transformed details in order to express his own ideas. Thus he emphasized the hero's supernatural origin, his gaiety and his supreme, birdlike isolation, all qualities which—as we can see—fitted in perfectly with Yeats' own long-standing theories. Thus, too, his imagery, though it retains some of the primitive fire of the early sagas, often becomes unexpectedly complicated and mystical. Echoes of *A Vision* persist throughout the plays and poems, and all the trappings of the original myth are infused with Yeats' personal preoccupations. Cuchulain's great value to the poet resides, in fact, in his ability to operate as a kind of "objective corelative" for a number of related theories and emotions. Ure notes that by means of myth, Yeats "unites the abstract idea with the personal passion and the personal meaning, and so resolves an otherwise frustrating dualism into poetry." And certainly Cuchulain, with his heroism and glory, was an ideal solvent for passion and thought.

Cuchulain, then, has many symbolic functions for Yeats, and the evolution of these functions corresponds in many ways to the evolution of Yeats' principal poetic themes. The Cuchulain cycle covers the entire span of his career as a poet, and even a super-ficial reading of the plays reveals the presence of most of the basic elements of his work. Nationalism, mysticism, heroism, all are combined in the one figure of Cuchulain, but they are combined at different times in different proportions. In the earliest work, for instance, nationalism seems to predominate; later, mysticism is clearly of paramount importance. At all times, however, each element is present, and each assists in transforming an Irish Hercules into a transcendent poetic image.

There are five plays in the Cuchulain cycle, and each is written in a style uniquely suitable to its subject matter. On the other hand Yeats wrote only two poems that deal exclusively with Cuchulain: the early poem "Cuchulain's Fight With the Sea," which is, in fact, a kind of companion-piece to *On Baile's Strand*, and the late poem "Cuchulain Comforted," which is, in turn, a kind of companion-piece to *The Death of Cuchulain*. In other words, Yeats envisioned Cuchulain in essentially dramatic terms. Where subjects more clearly mystical—such as, for instance, Byzantium or Leda—and subjects more clearly personal—such as, for in-stance, Maud Gonne or old age—could be handled exclusively in lyric poetry, Cuchulain's adventures demanded exposition in speech and action. Nonetheless, Yeats' plays were never con-ventional naturalistic dramas. He has been accused, as Ure points out, of "throwing over the real theatre in favor of stylistic poses and an hieratic attitude." And, indeed, he is often considered a total failure as a dramatist. Nevertheless, many critics feel that Yeats' plays—and particularly his plays about Cuchulain—are pre-eminently stageworthy, and that their neglect today is some-thing of a disgrace.

YEATS' PLAYS: T. S. Eliot once remarked that "There is no reason why a lyric poet should not also be a dramatic poet; and to me Yeats is the type of lyrical dramatist. . . . His early verse plays . . . have a good deal of beauty in them, and, at least, they are the best verse plays written in their time. . . . In the Four Plays for Dancers and in the two in the posthumous volume . . . [Yeats] found his right and final dramatic form. . . ." This statement is, of course, in direct contradiction to Henn's assertion that "it is curious to observe the unanimity of critical opinion that Yeats is not a dramatist . . . Aristotle would not have recognized his plays at all. . . ." While Aristotle's judgment of Yeats might, indeed, have been unfavorable, critical opinion is far from unanimous, and is, in fact, very much in conflict as to the ultimate worth of Yeats' plays. Eric Bentley, for instance, insists that "Yeats is a considerable playwright, perhaps the only considerable verse-playwright in English for several hundred years. Besides the solid achievement of his forty years in the theatre, Eliot's dramatic work to date seems merely suggestive and fragmentary. For Yeats composed dramas, as Eliot has not . . . he was able to start from a genuinely dramatic conception and carry it through."

Despite the assured conviction of Bentley's tone, however, it must be admitted that Yeats' plays present a number of problems. They are extremely unconventional, and often do seem to be more lyrical than dramatic in structure. They are all brief; the language is occasionally obscure; no character is ever fully developed as a human being; and they are all—particularly the Cuchulain plays—concerned only with "one moment of intensity, one moment of passion, round which everything is concentrated." As Edmund Wilson suggests, Yeats "is in reaction against Naturalism" and "has produced a theatre somewhat similar to Maeterlinck's. The productions of a greater poet, equipped with a richer and more solid mythology, these plays do, however, take place in the same sort of twilit world as Maeterlinck's—a world in which the characters are less often dramatic personalities than disembodied broodings and longings." Wilson finds, however, that this technique is detrimental to the plays. "Yeats' plays," he says, "have little dramatic importance because Yeats himself has little sense of drama, and we think of them primarily as a department of his poetry, with the same sort of interest and beauty as the rest." Eliot, on the other hand, agrees that Yeats is involved in "a reaction against Naturalism" and yet realizes that such a reaction, even when led by a lyric poet, does not necessarily preclude drama, and may, in fact, be more theatrically successful than Naturalism itself. Yeats, he says, "started writing plays when the prose-play of contemporary life seemed triumphant, with an indefinite future stretching before it . . . We can begin to see now that even the imperfect early attempts he made are probably more permanent literature than the plays of Ibsen or of Shaw, and that his dramatic work as a whole may prove a stronger defense against the successful urban Shaftesbury Avenue-vulgarity which he opposed as stoutly as they."

All of Yeats' plays are, certainly, potential drama of the highest order. Where he fails, however, he does fail because he is too much the poet. But when he succeeds, he is generally aided by his lyricism. In reading the plays, one must remember that his intentions and aesthetic presuppositions are somewhat unusual: he is not interested in characterizing, not concerned with complexities of plot, not driven to reproduce the speech of daily life. Rather, he is concerned with catching the essence of a dramatic situation and presenting it, as it were, in a kind of masque, with all the symbolic overtones that it demands. His dramas are not "three-dimensional" in the Naturalistic sense. They are, instead, stylized, oriental. In a stage direction for *At The Hawk's Well*, he prescribes a pattern of action for the Old Man: "His movements, like those of the other persons of the play, suggest a marionette." And, indeed, the movements of all characters in the Four Plays for Dancers, modeled after Japanese Noh dramas, are stiff and non-realistic. Yeats, in his plays, is interested, not in human details, but in the nuances of another world, the "artifice of eternity." He wants to set forth, on a bare stage with simple motions and masks, an indication of life, not as it is, but as it is in art. His plays about Cuchulain capture each "moment of intensity" to the full, and develop, in dramatic terms, themes that would have suffered if presented strictly in lyrics.

PLAYS IN THE CYCLE: The five plays in Yeats' Cuchulain cycle are, in chronological order, *On Baile's Strand* (1904), *The Green Helmet* (1910), *At The Hawk's Well* (1917), *The Only Jealousy of Emer* (1919), and *The Death of Cuchulain* (1939) which is, significantly, Yeats' last play, written almost on his own deathbed. The development of Yeats' style can be very clearly traced in these works. *On Baile's Strand* was conceived and written in the rather shadowy, almost pre-Raphaelite early style. Later Yeats revised it, sharpening and clarifying the language, so that it is now one of the most inherently dramatic of all the plays. *The Green Helmet* reflects his rising interest in Irish politics; the language is singing, more colloquial than usual, and the lines are long, reminiscent, perhaps, of Swinburne. *At The Hawk's Well*, one of the Four Plays for Dancers, is written in imitation of the Japanese Noh plays. Its mystical overtones indicate that Yeats has moved into the period of *A Vision* which, though first published in 1925, was a "work-in-progress" even in 1917. *The Only Jealousy of Emer*, with its emphasis on "the other world" and incidental imagery pertaining to phases of the moon, reveals the increasing importance of "the system" to Yeats. Finally, after a striking gap of twenty years, *The Death of Cuchulain*, with its searingly bitter prologue, its stripped, exact language, and its startling theatrical effects (a black parallelogram, for instance, is called for to represent Cuchulain's severed head), indicates that Yeats has passed into the final phase, the phase of *Last Poems*, where his old gaudy symbols desert him and he must return to the "rag-and-bone shop of the heart."

Yeats did not have these plays printed in chronological order; however, beginning with *At The Hawk's Well*, they form a coherent sequence of events, a string of dramatic "essences" illuminating Cuchulain's remarkable and heroic career. Before discussing the way in which Yeats handles his central poetic themes throughout the cycle, then, we will discuss the plays individually, in their proper order.

AT THE HAWK'S WELL: *At The Hawk's Well*, the first of the series, contains the seeds of all the other works. Cuchulain, young and splendid, arrives at the hawk's well, which is supposed to be a fountain of immortality, where an old man has waited fifty years for water. Three times the well has bubbled up, and each time the old man has fallen asleep. He is, as one critic noted, a "representative of the unheroic type, taunted by desire for the waters of eternal wisdom yet thwarted by fears . . ." Cuchulain, the hero, insists that he will be able to obtain some water. The old man points to a strange woman who crouches by the well. She is the hawk-woman, a woman of the Sidhe who frustrates all attempts to drink. As the well begins to bubble, she dances, and Cuchulain, fascinated by her "unfaltering unmoistened eyes" which "stare with inhuman subjectivity and ultimate wisdom" follows her, away from the well. The old man who has, as usual, fallen asleep, awakens to see Cuchulain disappearing after the hawk-woman, and warns him that "never till you are lying in the earth/Can you know rest," for this creature is leading him to ruin, to a combat with the wild women of the hills and a liaison with the fierce Aoife, whose son he is to kill in *On Baile's Strand* and who is to attempt to kill him in *The Death of Cuchulain*. The hawk-woman, too, will appear in later plays, particularly in *The Only Jealousy of Emer*. More important, the ideas inherent in *At The Hawk's Well* will appear and reappear in later plays. Birds, dancers, eternity and love—all these themes reverberate throughout the whole cycle. Cuchulain's search for eternity, a hero's search as opposed to the old man's dumb resignation, persists, and the hawk-woman's dance persists too, a dance that is simultaneously of life and of purification from life.

THE GREEN HELMET: In *The Green Helmet* Cuchulain returns from Scotland and from, presumably, his stay with Aoife, to discover that his friends, Conall and Laegaire, have gotten in trouble with a peculiar creature, the Red Man, who is probably a spirit from the Country-under-Wave. This gigantic person, clad all in red except for two huge green horns on his head, dared someone to cut off his head, and then, when it had been cut off, promised to return in a year to claim another head in return for his own. When Cuchulain arrives, the promise has come due, and Conall and Laegaire are quarrelling as to whose head shall be proffered in payment. Cuchulain manages to settle their quarrels, along with the quarrels of their wives, and, in offering his own head to the Red Man, proves himself to be the bravest among men. The Red Man bestows the Green Helmet upon him and he is declared the Champion of Ulster. The play is primarily concerned with Ireland, that country which was "made when the Devil spat. . . ." In sharp contrast to all the other plays, it is lighthearted and charming, but, again, not without philosophical implications. Life must be lived gaily, like a work of art, and Cuchulain is a hero because he does live thus.

ON BAILE'S STRAND: In *On Baile's Strand*, perhaps the most dramatic and completely stage-worthy of all Yeats' plays, King Conchubar, on account of Cuchulain's bravery and unruly temper, makes him swear an oath of obedience. The actions of the Fool and the Blind Man provide a continuous counterpoint to the altercations between Conchubar, who represents wisdom, and Cuchulain, who represents impulsive heroism. In the end, Cuchulain is forced to fight and kill his own son, begotten of Aoife. He learns from the Blind Man, who is a kind of horrible parody of Conchubar just as the Fool is a kind of horrible parody of Cuchulain, that he has actually killed his own son. Cuchulain, mad with despair, runs out to fight the sea, and is apparently "mastered by the waves." "Cuchulain's Fight With the Sea," an early poem, is also written around this story, but it is not half so effective a work as *On Baile's Strand*, about which Norman Jeffares remarks that "there is all the impending doom of a Greek tragedy in this play, the same tragedy as of the passionate Ajax, the obtuse Agamemnon, or the self-deceiving Oedipus." And Yeats remarks, in connection with the play, that "so did the abstract ideas persecute me that *On Baile's Strand*, founded upon a dream, was only finished when, after a struggle of two years, I had made the Fool and the Blind Man, Cuchulain and Conchubar, whose shadows they are, all image, and now I can no longer remember what they meant except that they meant in some sense those combatants who turn the wheel of life." This "wheel of life" is, in *On Baile's Strand*, seen circling around the problem of heroism, and its relationship to wisdom.

THE ONLY JEALOUSY OF EMER: *The Only Jealousy of Emer* directly follows the close of *On Baile's Strand* and picks up the story of Cuchulain's fight with the sea. He is thrown up out of the waves as an image of his own self, and though he is apparently dead, his wife, Emer, and his mistress, Eithne Inguba, attempt to call him back from the other world, the realm of the dead. Through the intercession of a spirit from the Country-under-Wave, the Figure of Cuchulain, who takes the place of the hero's body on the bed, Emer is allowed to see the Ghost of Cuchulain being tempted by a woman of the Sidhe, presumably the woman from *At The Hawk's Well*. She is told that if she renounces her love for ever, he will be returned to the realm of the living. Finally she agrees to do this, and thus saves him from the power of the sea, restoring him to life and to Eithne Inguba. Peter Ure remarks that "if *At The Hawk's Well* has for theme the heroic apprehension of life, *The Only Jealousy of Emer* is preoccupied with heroic values of love and death. . . ." Emer, in making her great sacrifice, has performed an act of ultimate heroism for which she will never be rewarded. *The Only Jealousy of Emer* is also concerned with the relationship between the realm of the living and the realm of the dead; a tension is set up between the two worlds that will not be broken until the conclusion of *The Death of Cuchulain*.

THE DEATH OF CUCHULAIN: In this last play, *The Death of Cuchulain*, the hero is given six mortal wounds by the kinsmen and followers of Queen Maeve, an old enemy of the Ulstermen. As he is preparing for the battle, he acknowledges, before Eithne Inguba, his gratitude to Emer for having saved him from the sea. She tries to dissuade him from going out to fight, but he insists. He leaves, is wounded, and returns. Aoife, whose son he killed in *On Baile's Strand*, binds him with her veil to a tree, preparatory to giving him the death-blow. But before she can do so, the Blind Man, that travesty of Conchubar from *On Baile's Strand*, appears and cuts his head off for a twelve-penny reward offered by Queen Maeve. The Morrigu, crowheaded goddess of war and death, whose presence has pervaded the entire play so far, arrives and presides over Emer's dance of sorrow before the heads of Cuchulain and his enemies. The whole drama is "mystical, death-haunted . . ." and, as Henn points out, "obscure because Yeats is trying to achieve a kind of desperate compression, working by juxtaposition of incidents in the hero's life which form a pattern at once too definite and too vague to be apprehended as a unity." Moreover, Yeats' final deathbed bitterness underlies every action in the play, from the Blind Man's Judas-like betrayal to the ironic closing comment by the chorus that "So ends the tale that the harlot/Sang to the beggarman."

COMMENT: When placed in a logical order, then, the five plays—with their companion poems—form a kind of coherent whole. Each work alone is rather fragmentary and incomplete; when seen in relation to the other works, however, it gains significance and an unmistakable richness of allusion. Cuchulain's fate has been determined from his first meeting with the woman of the Sidhe at the hawk's well. The plays that follow enlarge upon his nature and adventures, pointing always in the direction of his bitter heroic death in the final drama. Even together, however, the plays may seem somewhat eccentric and obscure, and yet a close reading of them reveals that they have an emotional logic all their own, a spiritual coherence that no amount of summarizing and explicating can reproduce in critical prose. Some thematic dissection, though, is helpful in understanding and appreciating the quality of this Cuchulain cycle and to enable us to see how Cuchulain is related to Yeats' Irish nationalism, his views on heroism, his mysticism, and his personality.

CUCHULAIN AND NATIONALISM: Removed from the context of Yeats' plays, Cuchulain is, of course, first and foremost an Irish cultural hero. Lady Gregory's book, published at the height of the "Irish Renaissance," employed Cuchulain as a symbol of the potential power and glory of the Irish people and of Ireland itself. And Yeats, who was drawn into Irish nationalism by his feeling for the rich Irish heritage and by his association with Maud Gonne and others, saw Cuchulain as the great Irish folk-hero. It was Cuchulain, he thought, "who stood in the Post Office/With Pearse and Connolly," and it was Cuchulain who inspired giant dreams of freedom in the Irish people. In *The Green Helmet* Ireland is seen torn by strife and dissension: "Here neighbor wars on neighbor, and why that is no man knows/And if a man is lucky all wish his luck away,/And take his good name from him between a day and a day." Conall and Laegaire, their wives and their servants, quarrel endlessly, and the Red Man, coming up from under the sea, can do little to unite them. Though he is, himself, an heroic figure, he merely serves to increase their misery. But Cuchulain, returning from Scotland to "this unlucky country that was made when the Devil spat," manages to unify the land again, and under his rule the Ulster men proceed to victory. Thus, in "The Statues," Yeats portrays Cuchulain as the spirit of Irish greatness:

> When Pearse summoned Cuchulain to his side,
> What stalked through the Post Office? What intellect,
> What calculation, number, measurement, replied?

We Irish, born into that ancient sect
But thrown upon this filthy modern tide
And by its formless spawning fury wrecked,
Climb to our proper dark, that we may trace
The lineaments of a plummet-measured face.

If Ireland was to be freed, Yeats believed, Cuchulain must be revived, must "stalk through the Post Office" bearing a face and spirit supremely beautiful in their ancient perfection of proportion. But "no body like his body/Has modern woman borne"; Ireland, overcome by the tide of the modern world, has become, like every other land, the home of "pickpockets and opinionated bitches." And in Yeats' view, only the possibility of a kind of "second coming" of Cuchulain's "great wrath," only the chance that his spirit may be renewed again in the spirit of the heroes of the Post Office, sustains Ireland, as a state and as a nation.

CUCHULAIN AND HEROISM: For Yeats, however, Cuchulain was more than a national hero; he was the type of heroism itself. Peter Ure remarks that "Yeats' inspiration and subject matter in the Cuchulain series were not the champion of Ulster but the nature and quality of heroism," Indeed, almost every one of the plays deals with some aspect or other of heroism. Jeffares feels that Cuchulain was "drawn probably out of admiration of Nietzsche's theories which were constantly in W.B.'s head . . . " and that, therefore, he is that transcendent hero, the Nietzschean "Übermensch." Whether or not it is influenced by Nietzsche, Yeats' version of the Cuchulain myth is certainly, as T. S. Eliot notes, "not presented for its own sake, but as a vehicle for a situation of universal meeting (sic)." Cuchulain, the hero, "burns the earth as if he were a fire,/And time can never touch him." His heroism consists in a combination of daring, gaiety, strength and beauty, and he is, in every sense, a free man, a challenger who, whether he win or lose a specific battle, is ultimately victorious over himself and over others. Walter E. Houghton summarizes Yeats' attitudes toward heroism quite succinctly:

Almost every influence of his early life drew Yeats to the heroic idea . . . Early in life the Mask he set up, at the opposite pole from the gentle dreamy Willie, was the heroic image as seen in Hamlet . . . It is the positive virtues of courage, love, physical strength, decisive action, and above all, abounding energy, that win our sympathy and form the higher law of heroic morality. It follows that the hero is freed from every form of hesitation, both moral and physical. Acting from impulse that is good, he feels, as Yeats says, an 'instinctive harmony,' a sense of joyous confidence and inner purity. Cuchulain 'seemed to me a heroic figure because he was creative joy separated from fear.'

In *On Baile's Strand* Cuchulain prays for power: "O pure glittering ones/That should be more than wife or friend or mistress,/Give us the enduring will, the unquenchable hope,/The friendliness of the sword." Of course, the will, the hope, and the sword are his, because they are his birthright as a hero and as a semi-supernatural being.

COMMENT: Yet the hero is never entirely complete within himself. Just as the Fool and the Blind Man are mutually dependent for strength and survival, so Cuchulain and Conchubar, the impulsive hero and the wise king, may need each other. "You are but half a king," Conchubar tells Cuchulain, "and I but half;/I need your might of hand and burning heart,/And you my wisdom." Still, in this relationship of wisdom and heroism, of reason and emotion, it is always the hero who is cheated by the wiseman just as it is always the Fool who is cheated by the Blind Man. It is always Cuchulain who kills his son, warned by his instinctive hero's heart to beware but blindly obeying the words of the king. The unheroic attitude is sensible and security-conscious: "O wind, O salt wind, O sea wind!/Cries the heart, it is time to sleep;/Why wander and nothing to find?/Better grow old and sleep." The hero, however, unless he is cheated of his heritage by the voices of wisdom, unless he succumbs to his own sense of incompleteness, wanders and struggles and does find, ultimately, the waters of eternity and the triumph of passion.

SELF-SACRIFICE: Perhaps the essence of heroism, however, is sacrifice, the lonely loss that may—and may not—lead to glory. "Here in Ireland," Yeats says, "we have come to think of self-sacrifice, when worthy of public honour, as the act of some man at the moment when he is least himself, most completely the crowd. The heroic act, as it descends through tradition, is an act done because a man is himself, because, being himself, he can ask nothing of other men but room amid remembered tragedies; a sacrifice of himself to himself, almost, so little may he bargain, of the moment to the moment." Yet glorious as this sacrifice may seem, it is invariably accompanied by bitterness. The closing lines of *On Baile's Strand* are an excellent example of Yeats' ironic double-edged attitude toward heroic self-sacrifice:

> Fool.   There, he is down! He is up again. He is
>   going out in the deep water. There is a big
>   wave. It has gone over him. I cannot see
>   him now. He has killed kings and giants,
>   but the waves have mastered him, the
>   waves have mastered him.
> Blind Man.   Come here, Fool!
> Fool.   The waves have mastered him.
> Blind Man.   Come here, I say.
> Fool.   . . . What is it?
> Blind Man.   There will be nobody in the houses. Come
>   this way; come quickly! The ovens will be
>   full. We will put our hands in the ovens.

Cuchulain, struggling like Caligula with "the ungovernable sea," setting himself against the indifferent universe like Prometheus, is mastered by the waves, sacrificed to his own madness, but the Fool and the Blind Man, describing the scene like a Greek chorus, are fundamentally unaware of his tragedy and glory and rush offstage to steal food from the untended ovens.

Emer too, whose sacrifice in *The Only Jealousy of Emer* is the ultimate heroic sacrifice since it is a yielding up of that hope which is dearest to her heart, is handled from this ironic perspective, though more subtly.

> Emer.   I renounce Cuchulain's love forever.
>   (the Figure of Cuchulain sinks back
>   upon the bed, half-drawing the curtain.
>   Eithne Inguba comes in and kneels
>   by the bed)
> Eithne Inguba. Come to me, my beloved, it is I.
>   I, Eithne Inguba. Look! He is there.
>   He has come back and moved upon the bed.
>   And it is I that won him from the sea,
>   That brought him back to life.
> Emer.   Cuchulain wakes.

Emer has shattered her own heart in order to win Cuchulain from the sea, but no credit will ever be given her. Eithne Inguba, ironically, imagines that it is she—who will reap the benefit of Cuchulain's return—that revived him, and only Emer knows the truth. The hero must contemplate his sacrifice in loneliness and without joyous recompense. *The Only Jealousy of Emer* closes with the repeated refrain "O bitter reward/Of many a tragic tomb!/ And we though astonished are dumb/Or give but a sigh and a word,/A passing word."

GAIETY: And yet, of course, the hero, faced with the necessity of sacrifice, does not give way to "lamentation and tears." Rather, his attitude expresses a "tragic exaltation of gaiety," a sense that life must be lived artistically and with sane persistent laughter. The Red Man in *The Green Helmet* is an heroic figure, the representative of "gay tragedy" as Yeats imagined it. Conall describes him to Cuchulain with awe: ". . . he stood and laughed at us there, as though his sides would split,/Til I could stand it no longer, and whipped off his head at a blow,/ . . . and there on the ground where it fell it went on laughing at me." Laegaire and Conall, both ordinary men, cannot understand or cope with such a phenomenon. "How can you fight with a head that laughs when you've whipped it off?" Conall asks in bewilderment. But Cuchulain understands; his impulsive heroism is part and parcel of such gaiety. He grasps the situation at once, and keenly apprehends the demands of honor. "He played and paid with his head, and it's right that we pay him back,/And give him more than he gave, for he comes in here as a guest:/So I will give him my head. (Emer begins to keen) Little wife, little wife, be at rest./ Alive I have been far off in all lands under the sun,/And been no faithful man; but when my story is done/My fame shall spring up and laugh, and set you high above all." Cuchulain is willing to sacrifice himself, and to do so with a light heart. His impulsiveness may seem foolish and irrational—and, indeed, he does exist on a level similar to that on which the Fool exists—but it is profoundly necessary. The Red Man sees it as an indication of his bravery and worth, and, setting the Green Helmet, symbol of supreme heroism, on his head, cries:

. . . And I choose the laughing lip
That shall not turn from laughing, whatever rise or fall,
That heart that grows no bitterer although betrayed by all;
The hand that loves to scatter; the life like a gambler's throw;
And these things I make prosper, till a day come that I know,
When heart and mind shall darken that the weak may end
                    the strong,
And the long-remembering harpers have matter for their song.

Cuchulain, though he be "betrayed by all"—as he is in the final play—will always be victorious, because his is the heroism of lightheartedness and laughter.

ESOTERIC ASPECTS: Cuchulain is, for Yeats, not only a symbol of Ireland and the archetype of the hero but also a semi-supernatural creature whose existence is aided and/or threatened by a number of supernatural forces. The unfolding of his fate is inextricably involved with Yeats' mystical theories and almost every play bears witness to the development of "the system." Even before Yeats wrote *A Vision*, however, he was interested in the shadowy Faeryland of Irish mythology. The women of the Sidhe and the Country-under-Wave are, in many ways, precursors of the spiritual realm he was to speak of later. And, throughout the Cuchulain plays, a tension is constantly set up between the other world—whether it be Faeryland or the kingdom of *A Vision*—and this world. In *At The Hawk's Well*, the hawk-woman who dances by the well is clearly a creature of the Sidhe. Her inhuman supernatural gaze calls to the supernatural elements in Cuchulain, and he follows her away from the water. She is, then, in a sense the "prime mover" of the whole tragic-heroic series: had she not gazed on Cuchulain and danced for him, he might never have claimed his spiritual inheritance. In *The Green Helmet*, the Red Man is, like the hawk-women, a character from another world. Again Cuchulain recognizes the power of the supernatural and because he does recognize this power and is willing to act in accordance with it he is awarded the Green Helmet. In *On Baile's Strand* the Fool, Cuchulain's grotesque shadow, is haunted by fairies: ". . . There are some that follow me," he says, "Boann herself out of the river and Fand out of the deep sea. Witches they are, and they come by the wind, and they cry, 'Give a kiss, Fool, give a kiss,' that's what they cry." And in *The Only Jealousy of Emer*, though the other world presented is, in many ways, more akin to the spiritual realm of *A Vision* than it is to Faeryland, the Sidhe appear again. Emer, who is shown the Ghost of Cuchulain being tempted by the hawk-woman, cries out "Who is this woman?" and the Figure of Cuchulain, himself a supernatural being, replies:

> "She has hurried from the Country-under-Wave
> And dreamed herself into that shape that he
> May glitter in her basket; for the Sidhe
> Are dextrous fishers and they fish for men
> With dreams upon the hook."

Finally, in *The Death of Cuchulain*, the Morrigu appears, after Cuchulain's head has been severed by the muttering Blind Man. She, too, is by now only half a creature of the early, more naive Faeryland, for Yeats has infused her speech and action with the mood of *A Vision*, but at least part of her belongs to the kingdom of the Sidhe. "The dead can hear me," she says, "and to the dead I speak./This head is great Cuchulain's, those other six/Gave him six mortal wounds . . . I arranged the dance."

DANCERS: The Sidhe are all dancers—the woman by the well, the woman who tempts the Ghost of Cuchulain, the witches who haunt the Fool, and the Morrigu who, though she does not dance herself, controls the tragic, senseless marionette jerkings of Emer, Cuchulain, and their enemies. Thus Faeryland is, for Yeats, a force that simultaneously thwarts, controls, and lures Cuchulain. Edmund Wilson remarks that he ". . . has made of this Irish fairyland something which puts upon us a stronger spell than the spell even of the folk-tales in his anthology. Yeats' faeryland has become a symbol of the imagination itself." And, indeed, Cuchulain's ability to dream and to imagine, while it is, in a sense, his downfall, is also an integral part of his heroism.

BIRDS: One important reason why Cuchulain's supernatural affinities are so strong is, of course, that he was begotten by a "clean hawk out of the air," Lugh mac Ethnenn, a supernatural being, "upon a mortal woman." Birds in general are often symbolically significant in Yeats' poems, and in the Cuchulain cycle they take on especially profound meanings. Yeats employs them as symbols of subjectivity and isolation throughout the play, and occasionally uses them, as he does in the Byzantium poems, as symbols of perfection in timelessness. The hawk, as Birgit Bjersby notes, is "particularly prominent in the Cuchulain plays . . . the hawk symbolizes both royalty and some secret divine power—not exactly evil, but dangerous for ordinary mortals to explore." Cuchulain himself is part hawk; thus, he is fascinated by the hawk-woman at the well of immortality and thus he is lured again by her in the other world. "Certain birds," Yeats says in his note to *Calvary*, "especially as I see things, such lonely birds as the heron, hawk, eagle, and swan, are the natural symbols of subjectivity . . . subjective men are the more lonely the more they are true to type, seeking always that which is unique or personal." Cuchulain himself, though only partly "subjective," never develops an immunity to the hypnotic eyes of subjectivity.

> **COMMENT:**   Yeats also associates birds with death: the Morrigu, goddess of death and war, is crow-headed, and as Eithne Inguba suggests, she alone "among the gods of the air and upper air/Has a bird's head . . ." In the strange poem "Cuchulain Comforted," the dead, in linen shrouds, put off their human voices and sing like birds: "They sang, but had nor human tunes nor words,/Though all was done in common as before;/They had changed their throats and had the throats of birds . . ." These birds of death are no longer symbols of subjectivity. Rather, the imagery in which they are described tends to be reminiscent of the artificial golden birds of Byzantium, singing in timelessness. Though these souls are not metal, not things created but themselves creators, they are analogous to the artificial birds of earth:

they are the "cocks of Hades." In *At The Hawk's Well*, though, Yeats describes the background as a "black cloth" with "a gold pattern suggesting a hawk." Here, in this pseudo-Japanese Noh play, where the actors are exhorted to move with the unreal stiffness of marionettes and where the hawk-woman stares from another world with inhuman subjectivity, the three symbolic levels on which birds exist for Yeats are fused: art, death and isolation shine forth in one flash of supernatural splendor, and Cuchulain, in whom these elements are constantly fusing too, responds, losing his human power and gaining his supernatural glory forever.

THE SEA: Like birds, the sea often has a special symbolic significance for Yeats. In "Byzantium," that "dolphin-torn, that gong-tormented sea" represents simultaneously human sensuality, religion, and the gulf that separates this world from the other. And Birgit Bjersby comments that "a breath of the sea blows through most of his Cuchulain plays, but it can be clearly felt that the sea is not only a feature of the landscape. It has a symbolic life as changeable as the sea itself." Always, in Yeats' plays, one feels the presence of a "misty moon-lit sea" beyond the rocks, or a wild tumultuous sea, whose waves master all humans. In *The Green Helmet* the fierce, laughing Red Man comes up from the sea. In *On Baile's Strand* Cuchulain, in his madness, is driven to battle with the tide. And in *The Only Jealousy of Emer* his wife and his mistress must win, from the vast, incomprehensible world of the sea, the mysterious Country-under-Wave. "Beyond the open door the bitter sea,/The shining bitter sea, is crying out," sings the chorus, "White shell, white wing!/I will not choose for my friend/A frail unserviceable thing/That drifts and dreams and but knows/That waters are without end/And that wind blows." "We're but two women struggling with the sea," Emer cries out to Eithne Inguba, and when, as a result of Emer's heroic sacrifice, Cuchulain is returned to them, it is only because the sea has, as it were, struck a bargain with his wife and agreed to yield him up.

COMMENT: All these persistent images and symbols, sea, birds and the other world, are linked together, sometimes very clearly, but more often in an obscure and inexplicable fashion, throughout the Cuchulain plays. The Sidhe live, for the most part, in the Country-under-Wave or in the air; they are birdlike creatures, supernatural in their subjectivity and inhuman isolation. In his half-death, when he has been mastered by the waves, Cuchulain drifts to the other world, beneath the sea, where he is taunted and tempted by that "dextrous fisher" the hawk-woman, who originally seduced him by the well of immortality. Death is, particularly in the earlier plays, subtly related to the condition of birds, and to another life beneath "the shining bitter sea."

CUCHULAIN AND A VISION: Yeats was preoccupied with the ideas that were to be most fully presented in *A Vision* from 1917 on, and perhaps even earlier. While "the system" appears very often in a kind of half-disguise in the images of sea and bird and Sidhe, it does too, appear directly in some of the Cuchulain plays, particularly the later ones. The aspects of it that are most profoundly related to Cuchulain's story are those aspects which involve character-analysis and those which involve the purification of the soul. Love, for instance, is seen in several of the plays as uniting those opposites termed, in *A Vision:* "antithetical" and "primary." In *The Green Helmet*, written before the system was entirely conceived, there is already a rudimentary suggestion of this notion. ". . . I am moon to that sun," Emer sings, relating the glories of her marriage with Cuchulain, "I am steel to that fire." And in *On Baile's Strand* Cuchulain further elaborates this concept of love:

> "I have never known love but as a kiss
> In the mid-battle, and a difficult truce
> Of oil and water, candles and dark night,
> Hillside and hollow, the hot-footed sun
> And the cold, sliding, slippery-footed moon—
> A brief forgiveness between opposites
> That have been hatreds for three times the age
> Of this long-'stablished ground."

The phases of the moon, too, as they are outlined in *A Vision*, appear occasionally in the imagery of the Cuchulain plays. In *The Only Jealousy of Emer*, the Ghost of Cuchulain, when first he views the woman of the Sidhe in the other world, cries out, "Who is it stands before me there/Shedding such light from limb and hair/As when the moon, complete at last/With every labouring crescent past,/And lonely with extreme delight,/Flings out upon the fifteenth night?" The hawk-woman who tempts him now is, in fact, an incarnation of the supreme supernatural beauty that is present only at the fifteenth phase of the moon, Full Moon. And, although Cuchulain himself is partly supernatural, her beauty is too perfect for him, and he cannot yield himself entirely to her, remembering as he does, Emer's imperfect human loveliness.

Finally, Yeats' theories about immortality, as they are presented in "the system," appear in some of the later Cuchulain plays. In *The Only Jealousy of Emer*—which is, perhaps, the most mystical of all dramas—Eithne Inguba says "Cry out his name./All that are taken from our sight, they say,/Loiter amid the scenery of their lives/For certain hours or days, and should he hear/He might, being angry, drive the changeling out." In *A Vision* the dead are described as undergoing a process of purification, one stage of which is "the dreaming back" where they recall their former lives and may even revisit the scene of life. *The Only Jealousy of Emer* takes advantage of this theory, and a good deal of the play is based on the mystical relationship between the world of the dead and the world of the living. In *The Death of Cuchulain* the dying hero anticipates the condition that his soul is about to enter. "There floats out there," he says, "the shape that I shall take when I am dead,/My soul's first shape, a soft feathery shape,/And is not that a strange shape for the soul/Of a great fighting man?" And in "Cuchulain Comforted," the dead hero walks among the dead, and puts off his armor so that he may weave a linen shroud like those they wear—so that he may, in fact, begin the process of purification, a process in which he will become "Hades bobbin bound in mummy cloth."

COMMENT: *A Vision*, then, exerted an important influence on the Cuchulain plays and on Yeats' concept of Cuchulain himself, whose supernatural origin made him an ideal vehicle for many of the poet's mystical theories. Although "the system" itself is not very often directly evident in the plays, it can easily be perceived beneath the gleaming disguise of birds and seas and an Irish Faeryland. Peter Ure has summarized the relevance of *A Vision* to the Cuchulain cycle very well:

> From the impact of the system on his poetry arose that set of symbols, almost of trappings, with which Yeats surrounds his poetic self, and from the system, with its curious mixture of allegory and spiritualism, of philosophy and necromancy, came the mythology of self. Few poets have gone quite so far in this direction as Yeats, and few have presented to the world poetic personalities worked on with such a degree of elaboration, rejection, and selection.

And Cuchulain was an important aspect of Yeats' "poetic personality." All the "trappings" of Yeats' mysticism were therefore brought to bear upon the conception and creation of every detail in his story, so that he exists with great fullness on the level of *A Vision*, a level replete with strange supernatural overtones.

THE MYTHOLOGY OF SELF: The "mythology of self" that Cuchulain represents is, however, not entirely confined to a mythology of Yeats' intellectual self. Actually, in many ways, Cuchulain was one of Yeats' principal public Masks, and a being into whom he projected many of his more profound private dreams and frustrations. Bjersby suggests that the Cuchulain cycle is, for Yeats, an "autobiographical interpretation of his own life." And, indeed, most of Cuchulain's qualities had great emotional significance for Yeats. Eric Bentley remarks that "to Yeats, as to Bernard Shaw, the histrionic pose, the theatrical mask, was indispensable." Henn, too, feels that Cuchulain's "heroism, love affairs, and fight with 'the ungovernable sea' appealed perpetually and most powerfully to" Yeats' "need for self-dramatization." And Yeats himself, though he does not comment directly on Cuchulain's personal meaning to himself, remarks in his autobiography that "I was always planning some great gesture, putting the whole world into one scale of the balance and my soul into the other, and imagining that the whole world somehow kicked the beam." Yeats' attraction to the heroic posture was enormous, and it is only logical that the Mask he should construct for himself would be, fundamentally, drawn in the likeness of a hero.

In other ways, too, Cuchulain's problems, and the problems of other characters in the Cuchulain plays, were simply reflections of Yeats' own concerns. In *On Baile's Strand*, for instance, Conchubar tells Cuchulain ". . . I know you to the bone,/I have heard you cry, aye, in your very sleep,/'I have no son,' and with such bitterness,/That I have gone upon my knees and prayed/ That it might be amended." Yeats, unmarried, aging and consumed by his passion for Maud Gonne, felt his childlessness very keenly and was, like Cuchulain, filled with profound longing for a son. On an even deeper psychological level, Richard Ellman maintains that Yeats suffered from an Oedipus complex, and that much of his work was concerned with the conflict between fathers and sons. Thus, in *On Baile's Strand*, the battle between Cuchulain and his son has, he feels, powerful emotional significance for Yeats. And Henn suggests that "from the Hawk's well onwards there is an intense interest in all aspects of virility and the contrast between young and old. The symbolism of the dry well and the old man watching beside it, need not be stressed; nor that of the girl who turns into a hawk." Ellman, too, finds that *At The Hawk's Well* is significant. "An autobiographical element in the play is difficult to overlook," he says. "The old man who has been patiently waiting at the well for fifty years is Yeats' intellect (he was exactly fifty at the time of writing the play) as the young Cuchulain is his instinctive self." At any rate, whether or not Yeats' undeniable concern with the problem of old age, his concern with his childlessness and his rebellious attitude toward his father are mirrored in Cuchulain's adventures it is, as Bjersby points out, "significant . . . that after a long silence on the subject, Yeats returned to the Cuchulain figure at the time when he felt his own death approaching."

DEATH: In *The Death of Cuchulain* Yeats' final emotional attitude toward the world is clearly present. The terrible bitterness of the prologue, spoken by "a very old man looking like something out of mythology" dissolves all doubts. The dying Yeats has returned to "the foul rag-and-bone shop of the heart" and, declaring himself to be in absolute conflict with "this vile age," cries out "I spit three times. I spit upon the dancers painted by Degas. I spit upon their short bodices, their stiff stays, their toes whereon they spin like peg-tops, above all upon that chambermaid face. They might have looked timeless, Rameses the Great, but not the chambermaid, that old maid history. I spit! I spit! I spit!" Yeats feels himself, at last, to be "out of fashion and out of date like the antiquated romantic stuff" that Cuchulain is made of. And yet, he is resolved, though almost drowning in bitterness, to teach, if he lives, "the music of the beggar-man, Homer's music." Cuchulain's death is made with such music, and after he dies, the dancing of Emer is "antiquated romantic stuff," the dancing of a goddess and a heroine rather than a Degas-chambermaid, just as Cuchulain's "out-of-fashion" life has been the life of a god and a hero, whose example alone may, in Yeats' view, salvage "this vile age."

CONCLUSION: Cuchulain, then, is in a very real sense "all things" to Yeats. He is a symbol of nationalism, whose name resounds with the potential glory of Irish freedom. He is a kind of archetypal image of heroism—brave, gay, and tri-umphant—and a supernatural being involved with strange mystical forces. In addition, he is a "Mask" for Yeats himself, a vessel into which Yeats can project his rebellion, his sorrow, and, in the end, his bitterness. And finally, as Ellman points out, this man who emerges from Yeats' poetry "is a modern man though his name be Cuchulain or Naisi. He walks a tightrope between false choices, he is torn by an inner division and undermined by preternatural forces which he is not in a position to assess nor has sufficient power given him to dominate. If he cries out his cry of the infinite power of man it is in the teeth of the facts not be-cause of them." And if, as Yeats asserts in *On Baile's Strand*, "Life drifts between a fool and a blind man/To the end, and nobody can know his end," Cuchulain accepts the inevitability of this situation with boldness and grace, laugh-ing in the face of death, and always singing, as Yeats did, "Homer's music," the music of eternal heroism.

CRITICAL COMMENTARY

EARLY FAME: Almost from the beginning of his poetic career, Yeats was recognized as one of the oustanding talents of his generation. Certainly everyone in Dublin was convinced that he was "a genius" when he was still in his early twenties, or so Katharine Tynan, one of his friends from that period, later recollected. And by the time Ezra Pound, with one of this century's keenest noses for literary value, arrived in England in 1908, he was convinced, according to Richard Ellmann, that Yeats "was the best poet writing in English," though "his manner was out of date."

In between, of course, had come many other kinds of recognition, most striking, perhaps, the popular fame the poet won through his writing of such slightly sentimental Irish folk dramas as *The Countess Cathleen* and *Cathleen ni Houlihan*. Then, in 1924, came the ultimate recognition—at least the ultimate official recognition a writer can receive in his life time: the Nobel Prize, an honor of whose value the poet, writing gratefully in *The Bounty of Sweden*, was certainly not unmindful.

PROFESSIONAL CRITICS: Professional critics, of course, have found Yeats—with his luxuriant allusions to be tracked down and his meaty complexities to be explicated—a perfect subject from the first. As early as 1931, when the poet was still alive, Edmund Wilson dealt with him in what is still one of the best studies available, *Axel's Castle*. Wilson brilliantly "placed" Yeats in the tradition of French symbolism out of which so much major modern poetry has developed (including that of T. S. Eliot and Wallace Stevens).

Also in this vein (of at least partially "historical" criticism) is Frank Kermode's much more recent study, *The Romantic Images* (1957), which, like Wilson's, sets Yeats, along with several other modern writers, in the symbolist movement. Kermode, however, goes farther than Wilson in tracing Yeats' literary lineage, for he shows the ways in which the symbolists and, more directly, the "decadents" with whom Yeats was associated in the eighteen nineties, evolved out of the early nineteenth century English Romantic movement. Another study which treats Yeats as an heir to the rich tradition of English Romanticism is John Bayley's excellent *The Romantic Survival*, which classifies Yeats along with Auden and Dylan Thomas as "a last inheritor" of that great spirit. More specialized, Hazard Adams' *Blake and Yeats: The Contrary Vision* (1956), deals, as the title indicates, with Yeats' relationship to his most important Romantic forebear, the early nineteenth-century poet whom he most admired, and whose works he studied most carefully (even to producing between 1889 and 1893—with his friend Edwin Ellis—an elaborate three volume edition of them, as well as "a memoir and interpretation of the symbolism").

Biographical treatments of Yeats range from "straight" biography to "critical" biography of the life-and-works variety. Joseph Hone has written a reasonable book of the first sort, while a number of writers, including T. R. Henn, Norman Jeffares, Peter Ure, and Richard Ellman have produced works of the second kind. Ellman's brilliant *Yeats: The Man and The Masks* (1949) is probably the best of these. It is one of the finest studies-in-depth of Yeats' intellectual and literary development to have been produced so far. Studies of various specific aspects of Yeats' work, of course, abound. Especially noteworthy are Peter Ure's study of the plays and Virginia Moore's *The Unicorn*, an analysis of the poet's esoteric thought and its relationship to his work. A good general study of the *Collected Poems*, book by book, has been made by John Unterecker (*A Reader's Guide to W. B. Yeats*, 1959). But, of course, innumerable other volumes have been written on all aspects of Yeats' poetry and personality. A representative selection of these can be found in the Subject Bibliography at the end of this book, together with more detailed information on the works already mentioned here.

JUDGMENTS: Judgments and evaluations of Yeats' total achievement have been fairly unanimous. As we have seen, he was recognized as a genius from the first, but most critics are also agreed in preferring the stripped "passion and precision" of his later work to the dreamier lushness of his early poems. Of course, an enormous number of differing—often violently differing— opinions and analyses of individual poems have been offered. But these have been discussed where they naturally belong, in connection with the controversial poems themselves. One of the few notable modern critics to have taken issue with the general accord on the body of Yeats' work as a whole, is the poet Karl Shapiro, who several years ago, in an essay in the *N. Y. Times Book Review*, classified Yeats as an "academic" poet, taking rather violent objection to his "obscurity," or at least to what seems to be the literary-academic establishment's exploitation of that obscurity. But Shapiro's objection, though it sprang from a good cause (Yeats' poetry has surely become the hapless text for too many pedantic classroom exercises), nevertheless missed its mark. Why rage at Yeats because "old learned respectable bald heads . . . all cough in ink," as the poet himself put it? The young—the young in spirit—in schools and out, can share his poet's passion still. And if his images or lines are occasionally obscure, that is because the images and symbols—the language—of the heart, whether spontaneous or learned through history, are often obscure, complex, richly clotted with feeling and tradition. Yet in Yeats' poems the masterful intensity of genius illuminates the heart's tangled darkness more often than not, lifting even the most difficult images out of obscurity and fixing them, radiant, into "the artifice of eternity."

ESSAY QUESTIONS AND ANSWERS
FOR REVIEW

I. Trace Yeats' stylistic development, locating, wherever possible, the most important influences on the poet's style.

ANSWER: As we have already seen, Yeats' stylistic evolution falls rather naturally into four distinct phases. In phase 1, the phase of *Crossways, The Rose, The Wind Among the Reeds,* and, to a lesser extent, *In The Seven Woods* (already a transition volume), the young poet wrote rather literary, mannered, ornate verse. He was much influenced by the pre-Raphaelites, in whose shadow he—like other members of his literary generation—grew up, and their dreamy idealism, their vague and misty, often sentimental, view of the world, became an important part of Yeats' first poetic efforts. This pre-Raphaelite influence was tempered somewhat, however, by the young writer's early—and enduring—admiration for Blake, Shelley and Spenser. Blake especially helped give his style rather more visionary fire, a rather tougher simplicity, than the styles of his contemporaries, thus making him easily the most outstanding among the group of hopeful poets who founded the Rhymers' Club in 1891. Some typical poems of this period are the dreamy, musical "The Indian to his Love," the idealistic "Rose of the World," the faintly sentimental "The Stolen Child," and the frankly sentimental "Lake Isle of Innisfree."

In phase 2, the phase of *The Green Helmet* and *Responsibilities,* Yeats' work became considerably harder, terser and more realistic, as a result of both personal and professional developments in his life. Personally, he had been deeply wounded by Maud Gonne's marriage to Major John MacBride. The wellsprings of inspiration, the romantic dream out of which he had written so much of his earlier poetry, seemed now to dry up in him. Shocked and bitter, he turned from his youthful, musical praise of the beloved to a stripped and savage consideration of harsh reality. Professionally, he had become increasingly involved with the Abbey Theatre, and the modifications play-writing had brought about in his style brilliantly suited the bitterness of his personal mood. The stage required precision of language, ease, simplicity, spareness. Under its influence Yeats' poems became much more conversational and dramatic than they had ever been before. The casual, colloquial "Adam's Curse" and the bitterly succinct "Fascination of What's Difficult" are two good examples of his stylistic development in this period.

In phase 3 Yeats' lines lengthened and expanded somewhat; his style again became more intricate than it had been in phase 2. Caught up in new occult speculations, his imagination unleashed (as we have seen) by marriage and work on *A Vision*, he began to write newly metaphysical poems which, however, were shaped with a "passion and precision" that had been lacking in the dreamy early verses of phase 1. Not only had his theatrical work permanently cleared his style of vagueness and clutter, but his relationship with the young American poet, Ezra Pound, had helped to modernize the somewhat old-fashioned, ornate manner of phass 1. Thus, though phase 3 returned to the richness of phase 1, it structured that richness with a precision learned from phase 2. Some obvious examples of the poet's great creative flowering in this period (which spanned *The Wild Swans at Coole*, *Michael Robartes and the Dancer*, *The Tower* and the first half of *The Winding Stair*) are "Sailing to Byzantium," "The Second Coming," "A Prayer for My Daughter," "Leda and the Swan" and "Byzantium."

Finally, in phase 4, the pendulum (or so it seemed) of Yeats' style swung back again to the terse, stripped "nakedness" of phase 2. Rejecting all his elaborate symbols, all his carefully constructed imagery, in "The Circus Animals' Desertion," the poet resolved to "lie down where all the ladders start,/In the foul rag-and-bone shop of the heart." He had come at last, in his old age, into what he called "the desolation of reality" and he shaped his style to suit that desolation. Not that he was grim or gloomy; on the contrary, he felt that the artist must approach all things—whether sweet or bitter—with "tragic joy," with a kind of defiant gaiety. Accordingly, he made his last works songlike and simple, but with the desperate intensity of one whose time is running out. *The Oxford Book of Ballads* was almost his favorite nighttime reading, and indeed most of his final poems were either fiercely musical ballads or Blakeian visionary utterances whose sinewy terseness also reached a kind of songlike simplicity. The "Supernatural Songs," "The Wild Old Wicked Man," "The Black Tower" and "Under Ben Bulben" all exemplify this final phase.

II. Identify and discuss Yeats' major recurrent symbols and images.

ANSWER: Almost every lyric poet must use imagery obsessively if he is to create a vivid and coherent body of work. He must, that is, allow his mind consistently to dwell with particular excitement on some few symbols which, for whatever profound psychological reasons, have taken on special significance for him. Yeats, of course, was no exception to this rule. From the first, there were certain images and symbols to which he returned again and again, and into which he constantly poured the manifold accumulated tensions of thought and emotion. The rose, which had a clear intellectual meaning too, was one of the earliest of these symbols; it stood, according to the poet, for the conjunction of the real and the ideal, the aesthetic perfection of the rose's shape paradoxically depending on the mortal, imperfect flower. But other symbols, which did not have such clearly definable meanings, were also present in the poet's work from the first. The wind, which spoke with the voice of the faeries, the voice of the ideal, calling mortals ever onward in their pursuit of perfection, was one of these. Another was stone, which, early and late, represented sterility and, paradoxically enough, at the same time eternity. A third was the tree or trees, which generally stood for life and fertility, in contrast to stones. All these symbols can, as we have noted, be found both in early poems—like "The Two Trees" or "The Hosting of the Sidhe"—and late poems, like "Lapis Lazuli" or "Among School Children."

There are a host of other symbols, too, which were of central importance to Yeats. These include birds, especially swans, (which usually represent the soul of man—cf. "The Wild Swans at Coole" or "Sailing to Byzantium"); the sea (which often seems to signify the unknown—cf. "Byzantium," "High Talk," "News for the Delphic Oracle"); the dancer (who symbolizes a perfectly integrated being, one whose body and soul are perfectly balanced—cf. "Among School Children" or "The Double Vision of Michael Robartes"); horsemen (who represent both the strength and pride of natural aristocrats—cf. "At Galway Races"—and the soul on its physical journey through life,—cf. "Under Ben Bulben"); houses (which stand for the grace of established tradition—cf. "On a House Shaken by the Land Agitation"); the moon (which symbolizes all the mysterious cosmic forces that shape man's destiny—cf. "The Phases of the Moon"); the tower and the winding stair (which are "emblematical of the night," of the soul's spiritual journey toward the absolute—cf. "A Dialogue of Self and Soul" and "The Tower"); and the sword and sheath (which represents the changelessness of the soul and the precarious physical life which must support it—cf. "My Table," and "A Dialogue of Self and Soul").

III. How did Yeat's lifelong preoccupation with the occult affect his work?

ANSWER: From the first, Yeats' interest in the occult, in esoteric research, shaped and directed his work as a poet. For one thing, his interest in the occult was a sign of his basic idealism, of the Platonism that was expressed—though without using occult symbolism—even in the first poems that he published. Later,

however, the influence of the occult on his poetry became more
direct. His spiritualistic contact with the ghost, Leo Africanus
(cf. *Per Amica Silentia Lunae* and the Introduction to *The Wild
Swans at Coole* in this book) eventually produced his theory of
Masks, which became central to his development as a poet. More
important, his wife's occult experiments, those experiments with
automatic writing which she undertook for his sake in the first
place, ultimately led to his construction of *A Vision*, surely one of
the most elaborate esoteric systems any poet has ever produced.
A Vision, as we have seen, had a tremendous influence on Yeats'
poetry, liberating his speculative imagination for flights such as it
had never taken before. Indeed, the poet later declared that his
invisible "instructors" had come to bring him "metaphors for
poetry" in the first place. Later in life, however, when the tide of
A Vision had somewhat receded, Yeats' interest in the occult
persisted. His "Supernatural Songs," perhaps the most successful
"metaphysical" poems of his last years, rely heavily on ideas
drawn from Swedenborg, Hermes Trismegistus and other esoteric
thinkers, as well as (still) on Yeats' own "system." And even in
his official "last" poem, "Under Ben Bulben," his poetic last will
and testament, the poet's imagery is drawn from esoteric thought.
Those "pale, long-visaged" horsemen, those immortal riders
through the Irish hills, belong not to the real world, not to the
past or the present, but to the shadowy half-realm of the occult, a
realm of which Yeats had all his life been an indefatigable explorer.

SUBJECT BIBLIOGRAPHY AND GUIDE TO FURTHER RESEARCH

I. PRIMARY SOURCES

Allt and Alspach. *The Variorum Edition of the Poems of W. B. Yeats.* New York, 1957. A "must" for the serious student of Yeats' poetry. Yeats revised all his poems—even his earliest—so extensively in later life, as well as in the first course of composition, that there are often several different versions of a lyric extant, and the critic must, certainly, know which one he is talking about.

Yeats, W. B. *A Vision.* New York, 1938. Also required reading for the serious student, for obvious reasons.

Yeats, W. B. *The Autobiography of W. B. Yeats.* Consists of several different volumes of memoirs and reminiscences which shed much light on the relationship between the poet's personal experiences and his work.

Yeats, W. B. *Collected Plays.* New York, 1950. This, and not the 1934 edition, is the complete edition.

Yeats, W. B. *Collected Poems.* N.Y. 1955.

The really diligent researcher may also wish to consult Yeats' *Essays* and especially his little book on Masks and Leo Africanus, *Per Amica Silentia Lunae* (available in various volumes).

His letters, collected and edited by Allan Wade, may also prove extremely useful and enlightening, and the Soho bibliography of the works of W. B. Yeats, also produced by Allan Wade (London, 1957) is an essential aid to research.

II. SECONDARY SOURCES

A. BIOGRAPHIES AND DEVELOPMENTAL STUDIES

Ellmann, Richard. *Yeats: The Man and the Masks.* New York, 1948. Readily available in paperback, this is a brilliant, lucidly written study of Yeats' poetic and intellectual development, one of the best such studies to be found anywhere.

Ellmann, Richard. *The Identity of Yeats.* New York, 1954.

Henn, T. R. *The Lonely Tower*, London, 1950. Contains much biographical material.

Hone, Joseph. *W. B. Yeats*. New York, 1943. The official "authorized" biography.

Jeffares, A. Norman. *W. B. Yeats, Man and Poet*. New Haven, 1949.

Parkinson, T. *W. B. Yeats, Self Critic*. Berkeley, 1951.

Stallworthy, Jon. *Between the Lines: Yeats' Poetry in the Making*. Oxford, 1963.

Stock, A. G. *W. B. Yeats: His Poetry and Thought*. Cambridge (England), 1961.

Ure, Peter. *W. B. Yeats*. New York, 1964. Part of the Evergreen Pilot Series, this is a brief, useful, paperback study of the poet's life-and-works.

B.   "HISTORICAL" CRITICISM

Bayley, John. *The Romantic Survival*. London, 1957. Traces the evolution of English Romanticism through the late nineteenth century and up to its modern re-vitalization in the work of Yeats, Auden and Dylan Thomas. Very interesting on Yeats' Romantic roots and background.

Kermode, Frank. *The Romantic Image*. New York, 1957. Relates Yeats' central ideas and images, through their Symbolist and pre-Raphaelite antecedents, to their origins in central Romantic preoccupations. Readily available in paperback, this is one of the most exciting historical studies of Yeats.

Shaw, Priscilla Washburn. *Rilke, Valery and Yeats: The Domain of the Self*. Rutgers, 1964. Compares Yeats to the major German and French poets of the twentieth century, finding important parallels among all three.

Wilson, Edmund. *Axel's Castle*. New York, 1931. Readily available in paperback, this is still one of the most useful studies ever made of Yeats' Symbolist background.

Wilson, F. A. C. *W. B. Yeats and Tradition*. New York, 1958.

C.   EXPLICATIONS AND ANALYSES

Engelberg, Edward. *The Vast Design: Patterns in W. B. Yeats' Aesthetic*. Toronto, 1964.

Jeffares, A. Norman. *The Poems of W. B. Yeats*. New York, 1961.

Parkinson, T. *W. B. Yeats: The Later Poetry*. Berkeley, 1964.

Saul, George Brandon. *Prolegomena To the Study of Yeats' Poems*. Philadelphia, 1957. Contains the best list of books and articles about Yeats that has been compiled to date; also locates the major critical studies of each of Yeats' poems.

Stauffer, Donald. *The Golden Nightingale*. New York, 1949.

Unterecker, John. *A Reader's Guide to W. B. Yeats*. New York, 1959. Available in paperback. A well-written, careful, comprehensive study of the *Collected Poems*, section by section.

D. SPECIALIZED STUDIES

Bjersby, Birgit. *The Interpretation of the Cuchulain Legend in the Works of W. B. Yeats*. Upsala, 1950.

Melchiori, G. *The Whole Mystery of Art*. New York, 1961.

Moore, Virginia. *The Unicorn*. New York, 1954. An excellent and thorough study of Yeats' esoteric thought.

Reid, B. L. *W. B. Yeats: The Lyric of Tragedy*. Oklahoma, 1961.

Seiden, Morton. *W. B. Yeats: The Poet as a Mythmaker*. Michigan, 1962.

Ure, Peter. *Yeats the Playwright: A Commentary on Character and Designs in the Major Plays*. New York, 1963. The only really thorough study of the plays to have been made so far.

Wilson, F. A. C. *Yeats' Iconography*. New York, 1960.

E. ESSAY COLLECTIONS

Donoghue, Denis, ed. *The Integrity of Yeats*. Ireland, 1964. Includes essays by Jeffares, Henn, Kermode and Donald Davie.

Hall, Martin and Steinman, James, ed. *The Permanence of Yeats*. New York, 1950. Available in paperback. Contains essays by such well-known critics as Cleanth Brooks, R. P. Blackmur, F. R. Leavis, Eric Bentley, T. S. Eliot, W. H. Auden, etc.

Unterecker, John, ed. *Twentieth Century Views*: *W. B. Yeats*. Available in paperback. Includes an especially interesting essay by Allan Tate on Yeats' romanticism.

NOTES

NOTES

NOTES

NOTES

NOTES

NOTES

NOTES